THANK YOU FOR YOUR SUPPORT!
JOHN DILLON
GRAND CANYON AIRLINES

The
Aviation Legacy
of
Henry & Edsel Ford

Timothy J. O'Callaghan

PROCTOR PUBLICATIONS, LLC

COPYRIGHT © 2000 by TIMOTHY J. O'CALLAGHAN

Proctor Publications, LLC
P.O. Box 2498, Ann Arbor, Michigan 48106
800-343-3034
www.proctorpublications@aol.com

PUBLISHER'S CATALOGING-IN-PUBLICATION DATA
(Provided by Quality Books, Inc.)

O'Callaghan, Timothy J., 1930-
   The Aviation Legacy of Henry & Edsel Ford / Timothy
J. O'Callaghan. -- 1st ed.
   p. cm
   Includes bibliographical references and index.
   LCCN: 00-135369
   ISBN: 1-928623-01-8

   1. Ford, Henry,--1863-1947--Contributions in
aeronautics. 2. Aeronautics, Commercial--United States
--History. 3. Ford Motor Company--Airplane Division--
History. 4. Stout Metal Airplane Company--History.
5. Airports--Michigan--History. I. Title.

TL140.F6023 2000   6 29.13'00973
                        QBI00-816

PREFACE

With the beginning of a new millennium many have looked back over the past hundred years and selected Henry Ford as the business man, entrepreneur, industrialist etc. of the century due primarily to actions associated with his Model T automobile which was also recognized as the car of the century. In none of the testimonials has anyone mentioned his ventures into aviation. With the nearness of both the 100th anniversary of the Ford Motor Company and the centennial of aviation, both occurring in 2003, it is timely to examine the impact of Henry Ford's contributions to aviation.

While this book centers on Henry Ford's contribution, his son Edsel must not be forgotten as he too contributed a great deal to the development of Ford aviation. When the Stout Metal Airplane Company was purchased in 1925 Henry Ford commented *"this interest in aviation is largely Edsel's idea and he deserves the credit. Airplanes belong to another generation."* However, while Edsel was quoted on Ford's general aviation plans on a number of occasions, it was always Henry Ford who made the specific announcements. Unfortunately we will never know how big a role Edsel Ford did play as he was a quiet and unassuming individual who advanced his ideas behind the scenes. He shunned the spotlight, seldom giving interviews and always deferring to his father in public.

This work has evolved from my previous book *Henry Ford's Airport and Other Aviation Interests 1909 - 1954,* published in 1995.

That book was written in an effort to preserve the facts and data turned up when I had the opportunity to spend several years poring through the Ford Motor Company archives in the Research Center of the Henry Ford Museum & Greenfield Village and collections in other local museum and historical societies in the Detroit Metropolitan area. By the time the book was published I felt I had found all the records in the Ford Research Center pertaining to Henry Ford and aviation. In continuing my research after publication, however, I discovered additional pertinent files tucked away in the most unlikely corners.

Most significant of the new information was that which proved the existence of a new *Flivver* airplane built in 1945 that was only hinted at in my previous book. Second was the discovery of the 50 volume set of the LaCroix papers which documents Ford Motor Company's efforts in World War II and third was the development of a great deal more information concerning the relationship between Henry Ford and Charles Lindbergh. In addition, continuing research has provided a better understanding of previously reviewed documents.

My efforts with this book have been to blend this new information and understanding with the activities of commercial aviation during this period. Hopefully the reader will find that this provides for a better understanding of the Fords' efforts and their impact upon the development of commercial aviation in the United States.

Please bear in mind, however, as you read these chapters there are many loose aviation ends as commercial aviation history has been woven into the story of Ford aviation. Not the other way around.

One of the important things making these books possible was the availability of thousands of Ford Motor Company aviation photographs and motion picture film of the period. Henry Ford established a Photographic Department in 1914 rivaling any in the world and most of the photographs and film survive today in the Research Center of the Henry Ford Museum, Dearborn, Michigan and the National Archives, Washington, DC. In addition, I acquired over 2000 Ford prints and negatives from the aeronautical archives in the estate of Steve Hudek, an aviation photographic historian who grew up during this period around Ford Airport in Dearborn, Michigan and City Airport in Detroit, Michigan. Many of Hudek's photographs were unique and many were Ford Motor Company photographs copied, with their permission in the 1950s, from the original photographs in the Ford archives. As a result, one of the most difficult, but enjoyable, tasks was selecting the photographs for this book from the thousands available. In revisiting the photographs over 100 new ones were selected as better representing the subject matter.

In the process of researching the first book, I discovered the hoard of Ford motion picture film taken by cameramen of the Ford Photographic Department mentioned above. Reviewing the many thousands of feet of this film led to the production of a 40 minute narrated video of Ford's aviation history entitled *Henry Ford's Aviation Ventures 1924 - 1936*. It brings to life what the book describes and is fully described in the back of this book.

Leading to a deeper interest in, and knowledge of, the Ford Tri-Motor airplane and Ford aviation in general was my acquaintance with Bill Larkins, author of *The Ford Tri-Motor 1926 - 1992*, and several other aviation books. My work chronicles the history of the Ford Tri-Motor airplane, only as it relates to the overall Ford aviation experience. Bill Larkins' book is the bible on the Ford Tri-Motor airplane and anyone with a greater interest in these planes should obtain his book.

A debt of gratitude is owed to the members of the Research Center of the Henry Ford Museum, especially Cynthia Reid-Miller, Catherine Latendresse, Linda Skolarus and Carol Wright for their guidance in sorting through the maze of files and records and their constant help and willingness to answer questions. Also my friend Gert Blüm of The Netherlands for information on Ford's European venture.

Thanks are also owed to those who reviewed the manuscript offering suggestions and catching errors that I missed. David Ostrowski, Editor of *Skyways* magazine, John Bluth, Michigan aviation historian and former Editor and Publisher of the Detroit Athletic Club's monthly publication and Sam Sturgis, World War II Navy fighter pilot, aviation enthusiast and a good friend.

Finally, Edison Institute, HFM, Ford archives, Research Center or Henry Ford Museum refers in all cases to the Henry Ford Museum & Greenfield Village. FMC refers to Ford Motor Company. All photograph bearing numbers are the original Ford Motor Company identification numbers and copies of most of these photograph can be obtained from the Research Center of the Henry Ford Museum.

THE AVIATION LEGACY OF HENRY & EDSEL FORD

The
Aviation Legacy
of
Henry & Edsel Ford

MICHIGAN

Marquette

Iron Mountain

Traverse City

Grand Rapids

Flint

Lansing

Kalamazoo

Ann Arbor
Willow Run
Dearborn
Detroit

1

HENRY FORD'S TRANSPORTATION EMPIRE

Early Aviation

While the railroad had opened vast new territories across the country, it could not, by itself, serve the growing needs of agriculture and industry, and local travel was still tied to the severe limitations imposed by the horse and buggy. The first successful gasoline powered motor vehicle patented by Carl Benz in Europe in 1886 had, by the turn of the century, showed promise of an era of undreamed advances in transportation, filling the needs of commerce and bringing freedom of movement to the individual.

Frank Duryea successfully operated America's first gasoline powered car in 1893. In 1896 both Henry Ford and Ransom Olds tested their first versions of a motor vehicle. In 1903, Olds would be the first manufacturer to mass produce motor vehicles, selling almost 5,000 of his Curved Dash runabouts, while Henry Ford would be starting his third and final automotive company.[1] Also in 1903, the first transcontinental auto race across the United States took place, requiring over two months to complete.

Just as the world was beginning to awaken to the wonders of the automobile, Orville and Wilbur Wright turned peoples' attention to the skies when, on December 17, 1903, they made the first controlled, powered, aerial flight over the sand dunes of Kitty Hawk, North Carolina lasting twelve seconds. These twelve seconds would impact the world as much, if not more, than the automobile, but it met with much skepticism and was not widely reported at the time. The Wrights, perceiving this feat had great financial potential and wanting to perfect their patent on this stick and fabric bi-wing aircraft, continued further experimental flights in secret before offering a demonstration to the public. The skepticism and lackluster interest in aviation in the United States at the time, as opposed to the great interest of Europeans where a number of Frenchmen had already flown, convinced the Wrights to make the first public demonstration of their airplane in France in August 1908. As a result, the first public airplane flight in the United States was made by Glenn Curtiss on July 4, 1908, in a plane designed and built by the Aerial Experimental Association, an organization originated and sponsored by Dr. and Mrs. Alexander Graham Bell. Their aircraft, while similar in appearance to the Wright airplane, used different flight control mechanisms and was powered by an engine designed by Curtiss. Curtiss, a prominent young engine builder and well known motorcycle racer from Hammondsport, New York, was destined to become a major airplane manufacturer and would cross paths with Henry Ford.

their war surplus planes and, of course, by Charles Lindbergh's solo flight across the Atlantic Ocean from New York to Paris in 1927. 1909 would also see Commander Robert Perry, in an overland trek, be the first man to reach the North Pole, eighteen years before Commander Richard Byrd, backed financially by the Fords, would stake his claim

Van Auken's plane with Ford Model T engine in 1909 represents Henry Ford's first venture into aviation. Patterned after the famous French Bleriot airplane, it was not a success. (HFM 0.335)

The first major monetary challenge to these fledgling aviators was posed by the <u>London Daily Mail's</u> offer of a prize of £1,000 for the first aerial crossing of the 25 mile wide English Channel. That challenge was won July 25, 1909 by Louis Bleriot of France, in a 37 minute flight in his mono-wing aircraft. By now, public interest in aviation in the United States had blossomed with thousands turning out to attend any type of flying demonstration. This degree of the public's interest in aviation would not be matched again until the barnstormers of the 1920's covered the small towns of America selling rides in

as being the first to fly over it. Also in 1909, the first mile of concrete highway was laid on Woodward Avenue in Detroit, Michigan between 6 Mile Road and 7 Mile Road which would eventually lead to enormous changes in automotive design. Nearly twenty years later, Henry Ford would have a similar effect on aviation by laying the first concrete runway for airplanes.

Henry Ford's Early Interest

Henry Ford, having started his third and final company just five years earlier, launched his inexpensive Model T automobile in October 1908. It was the car that would put America on wheels and quickly make Henry Ford the most successful automobile manufacturer in the world.

Aviation caught Ford's attention as it did others and he was receptive to a plea from Charles Van Auken, a young employee who had started with him as a floor sweeper in 1907, to help build an airplane. He persuaded Henry Ford to finance the building of a Bleriot type airplane powered by Ford's Model T engine. A Bleriot type plane was selected, as Louis Bleriot was making a great deal of aviation news in France, having recently flown across the English Channel. In addition, being a monoplane, it was simpler to construct than Wright's biplane. Van Auken was assisted by two other Ford employees, Charles Smith and Harold Hicks who, in 1926, would design and patent the first airplane tail wheel used on the Ford Tri-Motor airplane. Ford provided the engine and space in an unused building and had his shop employees make parts. Cost of labor was recorded as $875, about the same as the cost of a new Model T automobile. The airplane, reportedly the first one built in Detroit, was flown in 1909 from a Ford owned farm, but the Model T engine proved insufficient to properly power the plane. Even after extensive reworking of the engine, the power to weight ratio was never adequate to get it more than six feet off the ground. In the final attempt, the plane was caught in a sudden gust

of wind, causing it to crash into a tree on the Fort Wayne (Detroit) parade grounds, slightly injuring Van Auken and temporarily suspending Henry Ford's active interest in aviation. Most articles credit Edsel Ford, who was 16 at the time, with assisting in the design and building of this plane. However, his own comments in a biographical sketch provided to the National Aeronautic Association in 1929, states merely: *"Became interested in aviation in 1910 (sic) when the plane was built by Ford Motor Company with a Model T engine for power."* Although this aerial experiment with Ford's Model T engine proved unsatisfactory, within the decade, this same Ford engine would power small airplane kits being offered to the aviation enthusiasts by a number of companies.

Henry Ford's continued keen interest in aviation is evidenced by his trip in 1912 to the Curtiss Airplane Factory in Hammondsport, New York. According to Alfred Verville, a prominent airplane designer of the period, Henry Ford's visit was to encourage Glenn Curtiss in his efforts to break the Wright brothers' aviation patent monopoly. Ford believed the defeat of the Wright patent would mean as much to the advancement of aviation as was his own successful fight in breaking the Selden automotive monopoly patent the previous year.[2]

During World War I, Ford's interest was focused on aviation by the government contract he and other auto manufacturers were

Glenn Curtiss made the first public airplane flight in the United States in 1908, the same year Henry Ford introduced his revolutionary Model T automobile. Seen here with Henry Ford, Curtiss had legal problems with the Wright brothers' patent similar to those Ford had with the Selden patent. (Hudek 0.3633)

awarded, to build the Liberty airplane engine. Following the war, Ford-built Liberty engines garnered favorable publicity from naval and military demonstration flights. In May 1919, the Navy sent Curtiss flying boats, equipped with the Ford-built Liberty engines, on the first (in stages) transatlantic crossing from Newfoundland to the Azores. In October 1920, four Army pilots requested the Ford-built Liberty engines be installed in their planes for their 9,000 mile trip from Long Island, New York to Nome, Alaska. Pilots of both of these expeditions praised the Ford engines and, needless to say, both exploits received a great deal of favorable press which served to maintain Ford's attention.

Lighter-than-air craft were also making news in these early years as German dirigibles built by Count Ferdinand von Zeppelin had, by 1914, carried over 35,000 tourists without a fatal accident. During World War I, Germany sent large dirigibles across the English Channel on bombing raids over London and in October 1917, the Zepplin L-59 had carried over 50 tons of war materials on a 92 hour, nonstop flight of 4,000 miles. In spite of these achievements, the Zeppelins were not a military success but they did demonstrate the potential of the airship and Henry Ford foresaw their development as economical freight and passenger carrying vehicles. Ironically, Count von Zeppelin was more perceptive as he is reported to have remarked in 1917 that his airships were antiques and the airplane, not the airship, would dominate the future of aviation.

Following the war, the U.S. Congress had severely limited funds for aviation development by the military, so the report in the Army and Navy Journal (March 6, 1920) was of real significance. The Journal reported that Ford had proposed to the U.S. Government *"building an airship without a cent of money to be paid until the craft is finished and accepted"* and even then Ford would not amortize their initial costs on the first ship. It was further reported that William Mayo, Ford's Chief Engineer, stated: *"They stood ready to build a hangar to accommodate an airship 1,000 feet long, furnish all the necessary material and equipment, develop the engines for the craft, and build an airship without taking a cent of profit from the government."* Mayo went on to state: *"The Ford Company had a representative in Germany looking into the possibility of purchasing a German airship as a model or, failing that, to buy plans and hire experienced personnel to come to the United States to produce them."* Ford's costs for this undertaking were estimated to run about a million dollars each for a prototype airship and a new facility for production.

Documents in the Ford Archives on this subject are minimal, but on April 25, 1920, Newton Baker, Secretary of War, wrote Henry Ford: *"Press reports indicate that you are much interested in the construction of large airships for patriotic reasons - - - - whatever you do toward that end you will have the moral support of the War Department and material assistance to the extent permitted by law."*

There is no record of Ford making any formal proposal to the Government at this time, but just the possibility, as reported in the press, generated a marked difference of opinion between two Navy groups. One group wanted the Navy to do all the first building of an airship but the other group was convinced that no progress would be made in the development of these airships without the involvement of private enterprise and their capital. This later group felt that having private interests build the airships would give them a better ship, sooner, than one currently being built for the United States in England, and that the private facilities could be easily converted to military purposes in time of war. This second group would soon be proved right. The British airship R-38, built for the United States Navy as the ZR 2, crashed in August 1921 due to structural failure. Six months later, in February 1922, the Italian airship Roma, purchased by the United States Army Air Service, also crashed due to structural failure. Ford sent Mayo to Europe to survey the aviation field to determine whether Ford should undertake construction of airships in the U.S., but lacking encouragement from the Navy, nothing further came of these plans.[3]

The Fords' interest in aviation, while indirect, nevertheless continued. Anticipating the importance of commercial aviation, Ford had his certificate to do business in the State of Michigan, dated March 2, 1920, include authorization for the Ford Motor Company to manufacture and sell aircraft and airships. In May 1921, Edsel Ford subscribed to and became a director of the Detroit Aviation Society. In July 1922, Edsel Ford and William Mayo became Officers and Directors of the newly incorporated Aircraft Development Corporation, formed for the development of an all-metal airship. The following September, Edsel Ford contributed $10,000 to be used to guarantee the prize money for the Pulitzer Trophy Air Races held at Selfridge Field, Mt. Clemens, Michigan.[4] In 1923, Edsel Ford, having been elected to the Finance Committee of the National Aeronautic Association, undertook to solicit funds for the organization. The Fords were very much aware of aviation developments in the United States.

The influence of aviation in the mind of Henry Ford, who was always a pacifist until the United States entered a war, was revealed in an interview with the Detroit Free Press (April 26, 1925) headlined: *"Calls Flying Machine Blessing To Mankind."* They went on to quote Ford, *"The airplane will stop all future wars by being held as a sinister threat over the heads of those who would make war."* A not uncommon theme when related to major technological developments. Similar sentiments had also been expressed by Alfred Nobel when he developed dynamite and Hiram Maxim when he built his first real machine gun.

Public interest in aviation was greatly increased during World War I as a direct result of the headlines surrounding the exciting and dramatic exploits of pilots like America's top ace, Eddie Rickenbacker and Germany's great pilot, Manfred von Richthofen, and the Nieuport, Spad and Fokker airplanes they flew. The importance of military aviation became more evident as the war progressed and the United States embarked on a pilot training program. Fortunately, the war was over before most of these young men saw combat, but the flying bug had bitten many of them. At war's end, the United States had a surplus of planes, mostly Curtiss JN Jenny and Standard SJ-1 airplanes used for training. Originally costing the government $5,000, they sold for as little as $100 used or $600 new. To many of these young pilots wanting to continue flying, but with few aviation opportunities available to support themselves, these bargain priced airplanes were their salvation. They turned to barnstorming. Most of small town America's first introduction to the airplane came when a young barnstorming pilot buzzed the town and then landed his Jenny in a nearby farmer's field. Few, if any, of the townfolks had seen an airplane and they flocked to the field. They were amazed at the aerial acrobatics and the more adventurous among them purchased ten or fifteen minute rides for $5 to $10. This, when $5 was a day's pay. It was a time of aerial experimentation and adventure.

While the public was enthralled with flying, the development of aircraft was stalled. Most airplanes, although improved in performance, were still just wooden frames covered in fabric, not greatly different from the first Wright and Curtiss planes. They rotted, even with constant care and attention and the engines were less than reliable. Coupled with the daredevil antics of these barnstorming pilots, many fatalities resulted, receiving wide coverage by the press. The typical life insurance policy of the day included a clause canceling coverage at any time the insured was in an aircraft as a pilot or passenger. In addition to the excess of planes, there were thousands of war surplus aircraft engines in government warehouses. Who would be foolish enough to gamble the large investments required to develop new engines and planes in the face of this enormous surplus and the public perception of unsafe skies?

There were a few, and one was William Bushnell Stout, an extraordinary individual who had been active in aviation for many years.

Henry Ford's Renewed Interest

Stout was a pioneer in the United States in the use of the thick, internally braced, airplane wing. Internal bracing eliminated the need for the struts, braces and guy wires then in use, the effects of which Stout likened to *"dragging a log behind a motorboat"*. He also pioneered the use of all-metal in planes in the United States at a time when everything was mostly wood and fabric. In 1917, he built a traditional all-wood plane with the thick-wing for the government and, by 1922, had built a thick-wing, all-metal bomber for the Navy, the first all-metal airplane in the United States. (Hugo Junkers had built the first practical all-metal airplane with an internally braced wing in Germany in 1915.) While both of Stout's aircraft flew, neither was practical and he was out of money. In November 1922, Stout, by now well known in aviation circles and a prominent member of the Detroit Athletic Club (DAC), wrote letters to 87 leading industrialists, most in Detroit and most members of the DAC, in an effort to get at least 25 of them committed to aviation by investing in his new Stout Metal Airplane Company. The company was organized to build airplanes and to operate an airline of its own, as well as give financial assistance to other airlines.[5] Stout sent these prospects a series of twelve letters, each describing a particular phase of aviation or airplanes. In these letters, he promised them only *"that you will never see your money again"*. It was to be an investment in aviation and help make Detroit, Michigan the aviation center of the United States, just as it was the center of the automotive industry.[6] As a result of war profits and the fantastic growth of the automobile, there were a great many wealthy individuals in Detroit, and by December he had eighteen subscribers, each committed to pledging a minimum of $1,000 and a maximum of $5,000. As work progressed on his four-passenger, all-metal Air Sedan, so did his efforts to raise capital, and by December 1923 his target list of investors grew to one hundred. By April 1924, Stout had sixty-two subscribers including William Mayo and Edsel Ford who had joined this select group the previous December; (Edsel Ford invested $2,000. Henry Ford never invested.) The list would eventually grow to one hundred twenty-eight.

Stout formed the Stout Metal Airplane Company to design and build the first commercial all-metal airplane in the United States, but was limited by the types and availability of existing engines. In the early 1920s, World War I surplus engines were so abundant and inexpensive there was little or no incentive to develop new aviation engines.[7] By early 1923, Stout had developed his small 4 seat, all-metal, Air Sedan airplane, powered by one of the war surplus 90 hp Curtiss OX-5 engines. The OX-5 engine lacked sufficient power and was replaced in May with another surplus engine, a 150 hp Hispano-Suiza which significantly improved performance. However, the plane proved to be too small to be commercially successful and too expensive for private use. But Stout had demonstrated the practicality of fabricating an all-metal aircraft. In January 1924, Stout had started work on a larger all-metal plane. Financed by his successful solicitation efforts, he developed the Air Pullman, named after the comfortable and well known overnight railroad passenger cars of the day. The Air Pullman was an eight-person, all-metal monoplane powered by a war surplus, 400 hp, 12 cylinder, Liberty engine. The Air Pullman, named the *Maiden Detroit* (a play on words, i.e. Made In Detroit), was test flown in March 1924. This first flight took place at the Army's Selfridge Field, Mt. Clemens, Michigan, 26 miles north of the Stout factory on Beaubien Street in Detroit which was just across the street from Henry Ford's first factory. For months, Stout ran sight seeing flights with the *Maiden Detroit*, demonstrating the reliability and practicality of his plane, as Henry and Edsel Ford watched with interest.

In 1920, Ford had purchased the Detroit, Toledo and Ironton railroad to carry coal from his coal mines in West Virginia and Kentucky to his mighty Rouge plant in Michigan. In 1924, he purchased two ocean going freighters, the S/S Oneida and the S/S Onandaga, the first of thirty-one Ford merchant vessels to service his plants around the world. In June 1924, Ford sold his ten millionth vehicle and was still accounting for more than 50% of total automobile sales in the United States. Henry Ford was one of the richest and most well known men in the United States, if not the world, and the expansion of his interests from automobiles, railroads and ships into aviation was a logical next step.

THE COLOSSUS OF TRANSPORTATION
COPYRIGHT, 1925, NEW YORK TRIBUNE INC.

<u>Herald Tribune</u>, New York City - 1925 Reprinted in the <u>Michigan Manufacturers and</u>
<u>Financial Record</u>, Detroit, Michigan - August 15, 1925

Through his son, Edsel, and William Mayo, Henry Ford kept abreast of aviation and the activities of the Stout Metal Airplane Company. As Stout's all-metal plane progressed, Henry and Edsel Ford became convinced that the time was ripe to actively promote commercial aviation and their efforts centered on helping William Stout and his new all-metal airplane.

maganese and iron whose strength was greatly increased by heat treatment. In an article in <u>Aviation</u> magazine (October 1926), Bill Stout spelled out the advantages of this new composition. While pound for pound, costing five times as much as cold-rolled steel, only one third the weight in duralumin is required to obtain the same strength. In addition, there is a savings in material, labor

The Stout Air Sedan, the first commercial all-metal airplane built in the United States. Although too small to be a commercial sucess and too expensive for personal use, it did prove all-metal airplane construction was practical. Note the passengers standing close to the revolving propellar. (Hudek 1008AS.586.c)

Bill Stout's Airplane

The metal used in the Stout and early Ford planes was a corrugated aluminum alloy called duralumin. Duralumin, developed in Germany just before the first world war, was an alloy composed of 92% aluminum, 4% copper and minor amounts of magnesium,

and tool costs, because duralumin is easier to work than steel. But there was a downside. It tended to corrode especially when exposed to salt water. By 1928, The Aluminum Company of America (Alcoa) had developed a new process which grafted a layer of pure aluminum to each side of duralumin sheet.[8] This new product was called Alclad and it

Stout's Air Pullman, his second commercial all-metal airplane. (Hudek 1008.AP.2098.c)

offered the previous combination of structural strength, good fabricating qualities and light weight, while the aluminum coating provided superior resistance to corrosion. The importance of all metal in the construction of airplanes was very clearly spelled out in Ford's 1927 airplane catalog: *"No one, no matter how skilled, can inspect a piece of wood and tell how strong it is. Spruce should stand 40,000 pounds pull per square inch; but no one, by examining it, can tell whether it will pull 40,000 pounds or fail at 25,000 pounds. Its flexibility, too, is an unknown quantity; no two pieces will flex alike under strain. Metal, however, is a determinate: it is possible to estimate within 5% its strength."*

Bill Stout made the point more succinctly when he remarked: *"Any plywood plane after six months time will start developing a 'veneer-eal disease'."*

Bill Stout's first Air Pullman, the *Maiden Detroit*, was sold to the U.S. Post Office in December 1924, for $25,000 as a result of a crash landing. On a trip from Dayton, Ohio to Detroit, Michigan in October 1924, the engine caught fire, and in sideslipping the plane to extinguish the blaze, the engine died, forcing a crash landing. In spite of going through several farm fences, the plane suffered minimal damage to the undercarriage and none of the ten occupants of this eight person plane were injured. Edward Warner, an associate professor of Aeronautical Engineering at the Massachusetts Institute of Technology, who was on board to evaluate Stout's plane for the Post Office Department, submitted such a favorable report that the Post Office purchased the plane after it was repaired.

Stout's Air Pullman survived this crash. The Post Office was so impressed with the minimal damage caused by the crash that they purchased it after it was repaired. (Hudek 1008.AP.2086.f)

Notes - Chapter 1

(1) Henry Ford's first company, The Detroit Automobile Company, was established in August 1899 and folded in November 1900. His second company, The Henry Ford Company, was organized in November 1901 and upon Ford's resignation in March 1902, was renamed the Cadillac Automobile Company, managed by Henry Leland. In 1920, Leland started the Lincoln Motor Company which, on the verge of bankruptcy, was acquired by Henry Ford in 1922. *(page 1)*

(2) The Wright patent, like the Selden automotive patent that Ford had faced, was so broad that virtually every aircraft was covered, requiring the payment of a royalty to the Wrights. Ironically, the injunction against Curtiss, and the injunction against Ford in the Selden case, were both granted by Federal Judge John Hazel of Buffalo, New York. While Ford broke the Selden patent, the Wright case would drag on until World War I when the Government persuaded all aerial patent holders to pool their patents for the good of the country. Following the war, Orville Wright (Wilber died in 1912) sold his interest in the Wright Company and in 1929 it merged with Curtiss Aeroplane forming one of the largest aviation companies in the United States. *(page 3)*

(3)   Although no Ford records have been found, <u>Automotive Industries</u> (January 1926), reported that the Navy had rejected a Ford plan for an all-metal "Flivver" type dirigible to be built for $300,000. Speculation about Ford-built airships continued over the years with questions about the blimp Ford built or owned in 1946. In spite of Henry Ford's early interest in airships, he never built or owned one, but Ford Motor Company was the first manufacturer to advertise by blimp, when it leased one to launch and promote the 1947 Ford. A surplus Navy "K" type blimp, used during World War II to search for German submarines along the Atlantic coast, was leased in October 1946. The sides of the blimp were emblazoned with, *"There's a Ford in your future"* on one side, and *"Ford's Out Front"* on the other, and flew for the next two years covering the Eastern seaboard and the Midwest. *(page 5)*

(4)   The record setting, winning Army plane in this race used Ford Benzol fuel, produced as a by-product at Ford's River Rouge Plant. *(page 6)*

(5)   The Stout Metal Airplane Company made investments in Florida Airways, Western Air Express, Northwest Airways and Scenic Airways. *(page 7)*

(6)   This was no inspiration on Stout's part. Howard Coffin, one of the directors of the Detroit Aviation Society had written prominent individuals in October 1922, soliciting their financial support: *"As you have seen by the papers of the last few days, jealousy of Detroit as the probable center of coming Aviation industry - - - has prompted a vigorous attack - - - from Eastern quarters. Won't you join with us in putting Detroit first in this rapidly developing new industry, as we have done in the motor car business in years past."* *(page 7)*

(7)   In 1924, the U.S. Air Service had 11,810 surplus Liberty engines, sufficient to last them for 26 years and by 1926 they were offering the Liberty engine for $2,000, plus a $10 handling charge. By January 1929, aircraft engine development had advanced to the point that Congress banned the use of the 4,000 remaining Liberty engines in new Army planes. Planes equipped with the Liberty engines were considered not only uneconomical to operate but were also dangerous to the flyers using them. (<u>Automotive Industries</u> January 19, 1929). *(page 8)*

(8) The Aluminum Company of America (Alcoa) had received samples of duralumin from a German Zeppelin that had crashed in France in 1917. They were also given access to German patents seized by the United States Government. Even with the sample and patent information, Alcoa had trouble in moving to quantity production until several years after the war. *(page 10)*

2

FORD AIRPORT

Airfield

With the barnstormers leading the way, aerial surveying, crop dusting and flight training had developed by 1924 into the largest endeavors in commercial aviation and none needed established airfields, or fixed base operations as they were called, to function successfully. Passenger service, such as it was, amounted to an aerial taxi service flying when and where the passenger wanted and, they, too, needed little more than an open field. As a consequence, excluding several military establishments, there were virtually

When Ford Airport was dedicated in January 1925, it was hailed as the most modern airport in the United States. Stout factory is in the center with the Ford hangar to the right. (Hudek 1008.AP. 2153.b)

15

no real airfields in the United States. As an example, the airport in Atlanta, Georgia, now one of the busiest in the world, consisted of one wooden building and 287 acres of grass. In 1927 Hoover Field, located at 13th and Pennsylvania Avenue, in what is now downtown Washington, D.C., had a road running through the middle of the field that had to be closed to automobile traffic with railroad type gates manually activated when planes took off or landed. Few towns or cities had even considered the need of a landing field, much less something as grand as an airport.

The vast majority of flying of the period was performed by the young barnstormers, most in surplus World War I Curtiss Jennys or Standard airplanes that many had trained in during the war. They flew from county fairgrounds, farmer's fields or any open field in which they could land a plane and draw a crowd. There had been sporadic attempts to start regular air services, where a person would actually pay to fly from one city to another on a scheduled basis, but the public wasn't ready. Their perception of the safety of the wood and fabric airplanes of the pe-

Ford Airport in October 1927 with the name FORD spelled out in crushed stone 200 feet high. The buildings reading left to right: airplane factory, new hangar, old hangar, terminal. The Dearborn Inn would be built in the light area across from the terminal building in 1931. (Hudek 189.4885)

riod, formed by the widely publicized antics and resultant frequent fatalities of the barnstormers, did little to encourage air travel or for city fathers to contemplate the need for airports.

The only organized attempt to develop landing fields across the United States was as a result of the 1918 Post Office decision to experiment with air mail service. With the limited range of aircraft of the day, the Post Office copied the old Pony Express system with way stations for emergencies and refueling where they could hand the mail pouch off to a fresh pilot and plane. In 1920, with the establishment of the transcontinental air mail service between New York and San Francisco, 15 landing fields were established approximately 200 miles apart, with intermediate or emergency fields located about every 30 miles in between. But few, if any, of the landing fields and none of the intermediate fields could be considered real airports.

As Henry Ford watched these developments, Edsel Ford invested in the Stout Metal Airplane Company. Bill Stout had built his first small, all-metal Air Sedan airplane and was working on a larger version, but he needed help. The money he had coaxed from the local industrialists to establish his company had gone to develop his first airplane, and without better manufacturing facilities and a flying field, he would not be able to continue improving his airplane, much less expand his company.

Robert Walker, Mayo's secretary, drafted a letter in 1923 for Stout to send to Edsel Ford (through Mayo), so Edsel would have something definite to discuss with his father. The letter detailed the efforts Stout's organization had put forward in developing his airplane, including the fact they had 34 people already pledged to contribute $1,000 to $5,000 and pleading for assistance in three areas:

"First: The moral and financial support of the community and its big men.

Second: A place to do our work well, with a flying field close at hand.

Third: A motor development, connected with our work that will enable us to have a developed, cheap engine ready for production by a year from this coming summer."

Stout went on to state, *"The layout of your eight-cylinder radial should be an ideal one when developed."*[1]

Mayo passed the letter on to Edsel Ford stating: *"I believe that Mr. Stout's efforts have been of a high enough character to warrant giving him some assistance, either in cash, a free lease for a certain length of time of a piece of property, a free lease of some building we may not be using, or any other combination that might suggest itself to you."*

In March 1924, after his plane, the *Maiden Detroit*, was completed, Stout had complained about having to drag it 26 miles from his factory on Beaubien Street in Detroit to Selfridge Field in Mt. Clemens, Michigan for testing and demonstration flights.[2] This required that the wing be removed before the trip and reinstalled at the airport and, of course, the procedure had to be reversed for the return trip. Henry Ford had been kept abreast of Stout's activities by Edsel and Bill Mayo. Believing that air transportation was to be as important as the automobile, and watching the performance of the *Maiden Detroit* during the spring and summer of 1924, Henry Ford concluded that Stout's all-metal airplane was practical and was the best available airplane for commercial use. Deciding the time was ripe for aviation to shed its recreational image and become a business, Ford agreed to build an airport and an airplane factory for the Stout Metal Airplane Company.

Three sites with adequate land, in the vicinity of the Ford Administration building in Dearborn, Michigan were proposed to Stout and by July 1924, a site was selected. It was bordered by Oakwood Boulevard on the west, what would be Airport Drive on the south (now known as Rotunda) and Southfield Road on the east. When Stout declared it was the best of the locations, but the most expensive to prepare, Henry Ford responded: *"that doesn't make any difference. If it will make*

the best field, that is the one we will take."* The land had been planned for a housing subdivision for Ford workers and when Ernest Liebold, Ford's secretary, complained that $15,000 had already been spent developing the site, Henry Ford replied: *"maybe it was*

Ford's experimental eight cylinder aircraft engine. Although well publicized, it was never mass produced. (HFM 189.3377)

a subdivision yesterday, but today it is a landing field." Ford put 38 tractors to work for the next three months leveling the property for its new use, moving 75,000 cubic feet of earth while leveling and reshaping the landscape. Supervision of the construction of the airfield and airplane factory was turned over to Glen Hoppin, Stout's business manager, as Mayo claimed he had no Ford executive available to handle this additional task. Although Hoppin was directing the operations, Henry Ford was very interested in his new venture, making daily visits to observe its progress and, no doubt, offering constructive criticism. An early problem developed when the Michigan Central Railroad, fearing they would lose their right-of-way, refused to remove unused tracks that ran directly across proposed runway number two. This was finally resolved by lowering the tracks six inches below the runway. The tracks remained until concrete runways were installed several years later. In addition, power lines had to buried and, on one end of the field, many trees, one of Henry Ford's delights, had to be transplanted or cut down.

The site for the airfield consisted of 719 acres assembled from eight parcels Henry Ford had previously purchased. A short time later, 260 acres on the north side of the field were set aside for the Edison Institute, now called the Henry Ford Museum & Greenfield Village.

The airfield consisted of two grass runways which was typical of the period although many were just open fields with a windsock and a X in the center: #1 runway, 3,400 feet, ran northeast to southwest and #2 runway, 3,700 feet (later extended to 4,200 feet) ran northwest to southeast. Both were 75 feet wide. More than 20 miles of drain tiles were laid for year round operation and, though not normally operated at night, the field was fully equipped with flood lights to accommodate night landings when necessary. To identify the airfield from the air, the word **F O R D** was formed along runway #2 using white crushed stone 200 feet high which made it visible from 10,000 feet in the air. One of the many firsts for Ford Airport.

The field was completed in November 1924 and the New York Times (November 15, 1924) ran an article announcing the decision to call it Ford Airport. While Edward Hamilton, a Stout pilot, flying the *Maiden Detroit*, was the first to land on November 16, the airport was not formally dedicated until January 15, 1925. The dedication ceremonies drew large crowds and were highlighted by an aerial demonstration of 12 Curtiss fighter planes of the Army's First Pursuit Squadron from Selfridge Field, commanded by Major Thomas Lanphier.[3]

The airport was hailed by civil and military aviation authorities as the finest field in the United States and better than most airfields in the world. Three years later, Clarence Chamberlin, who had followed Charles Lindbergh's Atlantic Ocean flight by two weeks but had flown 300 miles further, landing in Berlin, Germany, declared: *"the Ford Airport stood next in excellence to Tempelhof Field, the great air terminal at Berlin."* In 1979, Martin Greif in The Airport Book comments on the opening of Ford Airport: *"Seven years after the governments of Europe established their first international airports, America finally had an airport of its own worthy of the name. But it took a capitalist's money to create it."* Private civilian and military planes were made welcome anytime, free of charge.

The best surface for a landing field, according

to a 1927 Ford sales brochure, was: *"Heavy grass or alfalfa, with plenty of roots to bind the soil together. It should be hard enough and so smooth that a motor car can be driven at fifty miles an hour over any part of it without throwing the passengers out of the seat."* Reality was quite different as airplanes of the

Indeed, after the first National Air Tour in September 1925, some pilots were already calling Ford Airport *Lake Ford*. Ford's Model T automobile had been built to run over the poor, rutted, muddy roads of the time and his airfield was beginning to look like those early roads. Grass fields were fine for the small planes of the early 1920s, but now Ford was making big, heavy, three motor, all-metal airplanes and they needed a better landing surface. In December 1927, the <u>Ford News</u>, an employee newspaper, announced that a 600 foot concrete runway was to be installed for testing purposes. It would be the first concrete runway in the world. By April 1928, a

The airport sign with gold letters 4 to 5 feet high was mounted on the side of the first hangar building facing Oakwood Boulevard. (HFM 189.2839)

day were not equipped with tail wheels or brakes. Tailskids, dragging across the ground, acted as brakes and in the process tore up the runways, especially in inclement weather. As early as March 1926, Major Schroeder, the Airport Manager, was proposing the use and layout of extra hard runways stating: *"I feel sure that as our planes get bigger and heavier it will take a very heavy tough sod to hold us up, particularly during the spring of the year or after heavy rains. We are already reducing our loads to 500 and 600 pounds in order to get out of the mud."*

contract had been let to pave 1,800 feet of runway #2, 75 feet wide and 7 inches thick. (By comparison, a runway built at Metro Airport, Detroit, Michigan in 1994 was 8,200 feet long, 150 feet wide and 17 inches thick.) By the end of 1928, runway #1 was completed and the remainder of runway #2 was paved in the spring of 1929. The cost was $90,448 and the contractors had to buy reinforcing rods and cement from Ford.

The 1991 Smithsonian air and space book <u>Aviation Milestones</u> states: *"Henry Ford's greatest contribution to aviation was in build-*

ing the first airport in the world with con-crete runways." However, it was not always that obvious, for as late as 1940, John Wood in his book Airports, a comprehensive study of the world's major airports, commented: *"It is quite possible that we are somewhat overdoing it in regard to the enormous areas of costly hard-surfaced runways that we are laboriously providing."* At the same time, Ford was laying concrete runways, authorities at London's premier Croydon Airport were reported as saying: *"Everyone knows that pilots prefer firm turf and that talk of paved airstrips is just that — talk."* Croydon would retain its grass runway until it closed in 1959. Europe's first paved runways were at Sweden's Bromma Airport in Stockholm, opened in 1936, but as late as 1940, the landing fields of the international airports of Tempelhof in Berlin and LeBourget in Paris were still covered by turf.

Years later, Charles Lindbergh related the story Bill Mayo told of how he had tried to arrange with the airlines flying into Detroit to use Ford Airport as a terminal. One Sunday, a large number of planes flew over the Ford house, which was close by the airfield, and Mrs. Ford told her husband: *"those planes oughtn't to be flying on Sunday."* In addition, Ford had gotten word that visiting pilots were bringing liquor into the airport. Ford, a teetotaler, issued orders banning alcohol in his airport. In June 1928, Ford Airport was closed to all Sunday activity. The decision to close on Sundays forced Stout

Air Services, based at Ford Airport and doing a brisk sight seeing business, to establish an auxiliary Sunday airfield 5 miles west in Romulus, Michigan.

Airplane Factory and Hangar

At the same time as the airport was being developed, Ford was also building a hangar and a factory, and announced in the July 1924 edition of the Ford News: *"For the purpose of encouraging aircraft development the Ford interests will erect a modern factory building devoted to research in aviation. The buildings will be used by the Stout Metal Airplane Company and the Aircraft Development Corporation."*[4]

Airplane factories of the period were, for the most part, whatever building was available, and hangars, if they existed, were quite often barns or canvas covered wooden frames. With minimal capitalization and every plane hand built one at a time, the thought of a purpose built building probably never entered anyone's mind. Early photographs of Stout's crowded workshop on Beaubien Street in Detroit are typical of what faced aircraft builders. With that in mind, one can understand Stout's remarks, in his book So Away I Went, when he relates his reaction when Henry Ford told him to design his airplane factory: *"Awed at the expenditure of even small amounts on such a precarious thing as aviation, we designed the cheapest type of steel and brick construction that would fit*

Interior of Stout's first airplane factory on Beaubien Street in Detroit, Michigan. Located just across the street from Henry Ford's first automobile factory, this facility was typical of the period and was 26 miles from the nearest airfield. (Hudek 1008.AP.2017)

the need. Very shortly the building was put up and we were told to move in on a basis to be decided later."

Hoppin relates that Mayo directed the price be kept under $100,000 which probably accounts for Stout's claim that they designed the cheapest construction. Several months later, Mayo advised them their rent would be $1,500 a year ($125 a month). A very mod-

est sum indeed considering they had been paying $500 a month on their Beaubien Street plant. The 20,000 square foot factory was occupied October 15, 1924. One of the most significant steps in airplane manufacturing to be employed here was the use of metal jigs for precision manufacturing necessary for mass production.

A combined hangar and airport operations

Stout Metal Airplane Co. This is probably the first building in the United States built specifically to construct commercial airplanes. William Stout could hardly believe anyone would spend so much money on such a risky venture. (Hudek 1008.AP.2087)

Stout's new factory provided all that he could imagine - a spacious interior and located on a brand new airport. The airplane shown is the second of Stout's Air Pullmans, the *Maiden Dearborn*. (Hudek)

building, 65' x 120', equipped with a 6,000 gallon capacity gas tank for servicing Stout's and visiting planes, was constructed near the new factory and occupied April 27, 1925. A large **FORD AIRPORT** sign facing Oakwood Boulevard was erected on top of the hangar in July 1925. The letters, 4 to 5 feet high, were wood, painted gold, mounted on a mesh framework and were illuminated at night by eight flood lights.

Airship Mooring Mast

Lighter-than-air ships were in their prime following World War I with England and Italy vying to duplicate Germany's success with the Zeppelins.[5] The Zeppelin

had range and carrying capacity exceeding any airplane as demonstrated in 1923 by the flight of the German made French Zeppelin Dixmude (part of German war reparations to France). Just as the first American-built airship Shenandoah was launched, the Dixmude made a 4,500 mile trip, staying aloft nearly 119 hours. Many, including Henry Ford, saw the airship as the workhorse of the future, carrying large loads over long distances not possible for existing airplanes.

This is the first hangar built at Ford Airport and quite advanced for the time. While rather small it too was a rarity, being built specifically for use as an airplane hangar. This photo was taken in April 1929 during the All American Aircraft Show that was being held in Detroit, Michigan. (Hudek 189.6341)

Doctor Hugo Eckner, manager of the Zeppelin works in Germany and the premier Zeppelin pilot, had delivered the Zeppelin ZR-3 (also part of German war reparations and christened Los Angeles) to the United States Navy in October 1924. Following this, he visited Henry Ford in Detroit. *"The next time you come to Detroit you should bring your airship with you"* said Henry Ford. *"I'd like to"* Doctor Eckner replied, *"but you have no mooring mast."* Mr. Ford replied, *"That's easy. I'll build one."* Unfortunately, the site for the mast happened to be right in the middle of what, Ford's secretary Liebold and the Wayne County Road Commission had agreed, was to be a 204 foot wide super highway called Southfield Road. Once again, Liebold had to change his plans to accommodate Mr. Ford. Indicative of Ford's belief in the future of lighter-than-air ships was the fact that there were only three airships in the United States available to use Ford's new mooring mast; the Navy's Shenandoah and Los Angeles and the Army's RS-1.

By July 1925, the Aircraft Development Corporation, con-

tracting through Whitehead & Kales had, with Ford workers fabricating most of the metal work, designed and erected the new mooring mast. It was the largest, most modern, and only privately owned, permanent mooring mast in the world. At the time there were only two other permanent, rigid airship mooring masts in the United States, both operated by the US military.

The mooring mast at Ford Airport was the finest and only private dirigible mooring mast in the world but was only used twice. Inset photo shows man at the station that controlled the new haul-down device. (Hudek 189.2949) (insert is portion of HFM 189.2939)

A unique feature of the Ford mooring system allowed an airship, once fastened to the mast, to ride freely on a rotating collar so it could always face into the wind and allow it to be lowered to the ground. With stronger winds, the airship would be lashed to large cement yaw blocks that circled the mast. These yaw blocks had steel loops imbedded in them to allow mooring lines from the airship to be fastened. The haul-down device permitted cargo and ballast loading, repairs and passenger disembarkation at ground level. Previous systems required passengers to disembark through the bow of the airship, entering a room at the top of the mast, and then be lowered to the ground in a small elevator. Either the haul down device wasn't

ship was moored. In any event, Ford motion picture film reveals the haul-down device was never used. The tower was a three legged steel structure 210 feet high with 72 feet between legs, designed to withstand 100 mile per hour winds. It was considered tornado-proof as the heaviest recorded velocity in the Detroit area had been 87 miles per hour. The foundation pedestals to which the tower legs were attached, were concrete blocks 12 feet by 15 feet, extending 12 feet into the ground and were designed to withstand a pressure of 205,000 pounds. Facilities at the tower included buoyant gas, gasoline, water, telephone and electric lights and it could accommodate airships of 10,000,000 cubic feet capacity. It was painted with alternate bands

U.S. Navy airship Shenandoah, on its way to Ford Airport, was torn apart by a storm over Ohio in September 1925. Another year passed before the Ford mooring mast was used for the first time. (Hudek 189.2997)

designed to work in all weather conditions or the designers had reservations about its practicality, as they also installed a five passenger elevator in the center of the Ford tower. The elevator rose to the 176 foot level with an enclosed stairway reaching to the loading platform to which the nose of the air-

of chrome yellow, black and white, giving it high visibility in fog as well as clear weather. Ford had been informed that the Navy's airship Shenandoah was expected to dock at the Ford Airport on July 4th, 1925 and an all out effort was made to finish the tower, including working men 210 feet up in the air on

US Army airship RS-1 was the first to dock at the Ford mooring mast on September 18, 1926. At 284 feet it was the largest semi-ridged airship in the world. (Hudek 189.3700)

At 7:30 on the morning of September 18, 1926, just a year after the Shenandoah disaster, the Army's semi-rigid[6] airship RS-1 (284 feet long, 755,500 cubic foot displacement) became the first airship to use the mast. It was the largest semi-rigid airship in the world and was commanded by Lieutenant Colonel John Pagelow.[7] Henry Ford was at the top of the mooring mast to greet Colonel Pagelow as he exited from the bow of the ship. The RS-1, made by the Goodyear Zeppelin Corp., Akron, Ohio, was driven by two propellers, each powered by a pair of the same World War I surplus Liberty engines used to power the Stout 2AT airplanes.

The Navy's Los Angeles, a rigid airship (650 feet long, 2,475,000 cubic feet), on a training flight for new officers and crew, visited Detroit a month later, arriving at 3:29 the morning of October 15, 1926. A crew of 30 ground handlers was on hand to secure the ship although an additional 150 men were available at the Fordson Plant in the event that the back-up ground landing equipment was needed. The Airport was brilliantly illuminated with all sorts of electric lights and beacons and a smoke flare was lit at the top

the mooring tower 24 hours a day. The job was finished on time but the arrival of the Shenandoah was delayed until September due to the fear of summer storms in the midwest. One of the main purposes of the Shenandoah's trip to Dearborn was to test Ford's new mooring mast, as the Army had ordered a similar one for Scott Field, Belleville, Illinois. In anticipation of the visit, Lieutenant Commander Charles Rosendahl had wired Major Schroeder on September 2, 1925 that, *"Department has authorized trip for Mr. Ford and Mr. Mayo to Bay City and return or to Lakehurst."* However, on September 4th, the Shenandoah, two days into her Midwest tour was destroyed in a storm near Ava, Ohio, about 75 miles east of Columbus.

of the mooring mast to show the officers of the Los Angeles the direction and intensity of the wind. The Pontiac News (October 16, 1926) reported: *"Harry Brooks, piloting the Ford Flivver plane, assisted in the entertainment of the crowd by flying over, under and around the Los Angeles, several times passing within a few feet of it."* Hard to imagine after the Shenandoah disaster. Although scheduled to stay overnight, an approaching gale forced the Los Angeles to depart early.

school to watch the mighty airship float overhead as she departed Detroit.

In a letter dated October 23, 1926, Lieutenant Commander Z.W. Wicks wrote Major Schroeder, Ford's airport manager, a critique of Ford's mooring mast. The comments in his two pages of critiques centered on inadequate field lights and winches with inadequate speed control for airship mooring. He also stated that the unique haul-down device

US Navy airship Los Angeles docked on October 15, 1926. It was a ridged airship 650 feet long. The Los Angeles and the RS-1 were the only airships to utilize Henry Ford's mooring mast. (HFM 189.3787)

Leaving Ford Airport at 3:40 P.M. she circled over Detroit and headed back to Lakehurst, New Jersey. She was commanded by Lieutenant Commander Rosendahl who had been the navigator of the Shenandoah when she crashed the previous year.[8] Unlike the sparse attendance during the visit of the Army's RS-1, the Los Angeles received a tumultuous welcome by the crowds at Ford Airport. People today still recall being let out of

was a serious handicap and should be removed. He was further concerned with availability of a fixed ground crew fully trained and available for mooring work instead of the untrained pickup crew from Ford's huge Rouge plant. Wicks comments must have jolted the Ford organization, as Fred Lamkey, Ford's mooring master and former mooring master at the Lakehurst Naval Station agreed. In a letter dated November 10, 1926, Lamkey stated: *"The Ford Mooring Tower, though the latest, most expensive and finest looking, is inferior to any in the country."* He then went on to explain why, citing most of the same concerns Wicks mentioned, particularly the haul down device.

The Army's RS-1 and the Navy's Los Angeles would be the only airships to use the Ford mooring mast, and only on these two occasions, before it was dismantled just 20 years later in October 1946.

Sperry Beacon

By July 1925, a 450,000,000 candlepower Sperry Beacon searchlight, similar to those in use by the U.S. Air Mail Service for night flying, was installed on the southeast corner of the hangar. Tests by the U.S. Air Mail Service, who had installed these lights every ten miles from New York to California, determined that it was visible for 100 miles at an altitude of 700 feet, and up to 130 miles under optimum conditions. In fact, the flashing beam was plainly visible at dusk, ninety miles away, to the crowds at the dedication of the new Cleveland Municipal Airport in July 1925. The beacon, with a 36 inch diameter lens, *"produced more light than the*

Henry Ford with Admiral William Moffett (left) head of the Navy's Bureau of Aeronautics and Lieutenant Commander Charles Rosendahl, Commander of the airship Los Angeles. Rosendahl was the base commander at Lakehurst, New Jersey in 1937 when the German Zeppelin *Hindenburg* burst into flames and crashed. (HFM 189.3765)

headlights of all the 9,000,000 Ford cars then in operation. — The beam is of such intense heat that it may cause paper to burn several feet from the lens. — This light is the nearest approach to intensity of that coming from the sun yet to be produced." Ford News (July 1, 1925).

The beacon, 36 inches in diameter, was set to provide a continuous revolving beacon, but could be revolved and tilted through any angle. The plain lens, which threw a concentrated shaft of light, could be replaced by a dispersion lens which would spread the rays over an area one quarter mile wide by one half mile long, illuminating the landing field as if it were day.

Operations

Although built by Henry Ford, the airplane factory was run by Bill Stout and his employees as Edsel Ford held only a minor interest in the Stout Metal Airplane Company. The overall responsibility of managing Ford aviation interests, primarily the airport at this time, was vested in William Mayo along with his many other responsibilities. For the operation of the airport and hangar, the most highly qualified and experienced personnel were sought. Major Rudolph "Shorty" Schroeder (6'2"), the Army's chief test pilot at McCook Field, Dayton, Ohio and one of the premier pilots in the United States, was appointed the first airport manager and chief test pilot in May 1925. Major Schroeder had set a number of world altitude records, developed the first parachute flare, pioneered the development of night flying and was the chief test pilot of the airplane supercharger that would be used in World War II. His staff consisted of three pilots; Leroy Manning, Edward Hamilton and William DeWald, two assistant pilots; Cecil Sinclair and Dean Burford, three mechanics; Harry Russell, C. Bradley and H. West and two janitors and a clerk. On November 6, 1926 Schroeder was abruptly replaced by Edward Hamilton, the senior Ford pilot. An <u>Aero Digest</u> article (December 1926) reported that Schroeder: *"had his head lopped off due to the fact he differed in his estimates of the performance that could be expected of the Ford Tri-Motor, when only two of its three motors are working."* Apparently he was too outspoken for the Fords.[9]

Edward Hamilton left Ford in November 1928 to fly for himself and was replaced, as manager, by Leroy Manning. Manning ran the airport operations until his death in the crash of the Ford experimental bomber

XB906 on September 19, 1931. He was followed by Harry Russell, a former Army pilot who had been hired as one of the original Ford airplane mechanics and who had, by January 1926, been promoted to pilot. Russell

Major Rudolph "Shorty" Schroeder as a young U.S. Army Lieutenant. Schroeder had been one of the Army's finest test pilots establishing many aerial records before being hired to manage Henry Ford's new airport. (Robert Baron collection)

worked his way up to senior pilot, and along the way won the 1930 and 1931 National Air Tours in a Ford Tri-Motor. After the Ford Airplane Division closed, Russell was one of the few supervisory employees to continue working for Ford, retiring in January 1968.

Notes - Chapter 2

(1) In October 1925, Ford did announce an X type air-cooled airplane engine to newsmen but it was never developed beyond the prototype stage. Henry Ford and William Mayo continued to make comments about planned aviation projects, most of which never became a reality. *(page 17)*

(2) In 1914, Joy Aviation Field was developed as a small private airfield near Mt. Clemens, Michigan by Henry Joy, a prominent industrialist. Later used by the Packard Motor Company as a test field, it was acquired by the U.S. Government in 1917 for an elementary pilot training school. It was enlarged, improved and renamed Selfridge Field in honor of Lieutenant Thomas Selfridge, the first person to die in an airplane crash. It would remain the only airfield worthy of the name in the Detroit metropolitan area until Ford Airport was opened in 1925. *(page 18)*

(3) Major Lanphier had been appointed base Commandant of Selfridge in 1924. He took every opportunity to promote Army aviation, and the many happenings at Ford Airport offered the Army Air Service great exposure. He became close to Henry Ford as evidenced by the Ford Sport Coupe given him when he left the Army in April 1928. In April 1943, his son, Captain Thomas Lanphier, participated in a secret Army Air Corps' long distance flight that intercepted and shot down the airplane carrying Admiral Isoroku Yamamoto, the planner of the Pearl Harbor raid. *(page 19)*

(4) The Aircraft Development Corporation had been formed in 1922, with Edsel Ford, William Mayo and William Stout among the many Detroit dignitaries as officers, to develop the first lighter-than-air ship with an all-metal gas envelope for commercial use. In 1929 they built the ZMC-2 for the U.S. Navy, the only successful metal-clad rigid airship ever made in the United States. A small stubby airship, 149 feet 5 inches long with a displacement of 202,200 cubic feet, it was made of Alclad, the same material as the Ford Tri-Motor airplane. The Aircraft Development Corporation never utilized the Ford factory, although Ford workers did fabricate the airship's gondola and its eight fins. The ZMC-2 was decommissioned by the Navy in 1941. *(page 21)*

(5) By the end of World War I, Germany had built 135 rigid airships. Great Britain had built eight and France one. The United States built its first airship, the Shenandoah, in 1923. The only other airships built by the United States were the all-metal ZMC-2 in

1929, the Akron in 1931 and the Macon in 1933. All the U.S. built airships except for the ZMC 2 were destroyed by storms. *(page 23)*

(6) The shape of the RS-1, a semi-rigid airship, was maintained by a metal keel running the length of the ship and the pressure of the gas it contained. The Los Angeles was a rigid airship with the shape being maintained by an interior metal frame. *(page 26)*

(7) Lieutenant Colonel Pagelow, Commanding Officer of Scott Field, Belleville, Illinois, the Army's only lighter-than-air station, had been in charge of all lighter-than-air craft in Europe during World War I. *(page 26)*

(8) Lieutenant Commander Rosendahl was the Commanding Officer of the Lakehurst Naval Air Station in New Jersey when the *Hindenburg* exploded in flames in 1937. Ironically <u>Automotive Industries </u>(September 9, 1926) had quoted Rosendahl as describing Lakehurst as: *"a place which is altogether unsuitable for airship operations."* After having commanded the heavy cruiser Minneapolis during the battle for Guadalcanal in World War II, Rosendahl was promoted to Rear Admiral and became Chief, Airship Training and Experimentation for the Navy. *(page 27)*

(9) After being fired by Ford, Major Schroeder went on to many important positions in aviation, most memorable among them being his participation as the Assistant Director of the Bureau of Air Commerce in the investigation of the Zeppelin *Hindenburg* disaster in 1937. He ended his career as Vice President of Safety for United Air Lines. *(page 29)*

3

FORD AIR TRANSPORT SERVICE

First Scheduled Air Service

Following World War I, European governments, reflecting on the influence of aviation during the war and as concerned with the next war in Europe as they were with advancing aviation, provided heavy subsidies to develop their aviation industry. In an interview with Aviation magazine (August 17, 1925) M. Henri Bouche, editor of the prominent French magazine L'Aeronautique stated: *"The French government believes that aviation is of the greatest importance to the future security and commercial prosperity of the republic."* Further, *"We are doing everything possssible, through direct subsidies, and through the establishment and maintenance of landing fields, night flying beacons and radio stations, and the provision of weather reports to stimulate commercial aviation."* In addition: *"Our law provides for the regulation of air traffic - the inspection of pilots, fields and equipment."*

Bulletins of The Daniel Guggenheim Fund for the Promotion of Aeronautics[1] detail the large subsidies being given to the British and German airlines as late as 1928 and explains how both countries had merged all of their independent passenger air operations under their respective state airlines, eliminating most internal competition.

The United States government, insulated from Europe by the Atlantic Ocean and having been spared the devastating effects of the war, reacted differently. The government was adamant in its refusal to subsidize private enterprise. The predictable result was there was no organized air service in the United States even in view of the United States' poor aviation record in the recent war. So anemic had America's aviation industry been in 1917, that virtually all planes used by American pilots in Europe during World War I were built by the English or French. However, even those opposed to direct subsidies admitted the military value of civilian aviation in regards to the pool of trained pilots it created, as well as the benefits of having a developed aviation industry in time of war. But it would take time for the legislatures to understand the needs and potential of commercial aviation.

The itinerant barnstormer or gypsy flyer, as

they were also known, was largely responsible for bringing aviation to the small towns in the heartland of America. Without them, most people of the times would have never seen an airplane much less ride in one. They were, in effect, the pioneers of commercial aviation. Unfortunately, pilots needed neither licenses for themselves or their airplanes, and the old surplus World War I aircraft they were using, built to last a matter of months in combat, were wearing out. Along with wing walkers and daredevil parachutists, these gypsy flyers had many fatal accidents that inevitably made the front page of the local and many times national newspapers. The Gates Flying Circus, probably the most famous and one of the few organized groups of barnstormers at the time, reflects the deadliness of this occupation. In the seven years they were operational, 28 pilots and 20 stuntmen flew for them. 16 of the pilots and 10 of the stuntment would eventualy die in aerial accidents. The result was a perception that aviation was an extremely dangerous

Ford flight mechanic Harry Russel and pilot Eddie Hamilton ready to inaugurate the Ford Air Transportation Service between Detroit, Michigan and Chicago, Illinois on April 13, 1925. Both became managers of Ford Airport. (HFM 833.41670)

pastime and had little future, a belief reinforced by the fact that no rules or regulations existed to govern it. It was hard to take this flying game seriously if the government didn't think it important enough to impose even modest regulations.

There were, however, farsighted and influential people, working behind the scenes, urging rules to restrict the barnstormers and establish other rudimentary regulations as well as providing indirect government participation in the industry. In spite of the lawmakers' reluctance to aid aviation, the precedent of government assistance and participation in transportation was well established. The government had provided a navigation system for shipping, an enormous road system for the automobile and had made land grants of over 155,000,000 acres to the railroads along with attendant regulations for all three of these transportation modes. Aviation needed some of the same. The most important needs included some sort of licensing to insure the saftey of the aircraft and the competence of the aviator; an aerial navigation system — a lost pilot could find out where he was only by landing in a field and asking the nearby farmer or flying dangerously close licensed in one state could not necessarily fly into the air space of another state, providing that is, that the other state had any laws at all. In 1926, only 19 of the 48 states had any aviation laws according to the Aero-

Stout's first Air Transport built in the new factory provided by Henry Ford. A new Ford Air Transport Service truck is loading the plane for its first flight to Chicago. Sign on the airplane tail reads *"Maiden Dearborn, Ford Airport of Dearborn."* (Hudek 833.41620)

to the railroad station to read the name sign on the side of the building; and regulations which would establish responsibilities so that insurance underwriting could be calculated and legal decisions rendered. For instance, what were the responsibilities of manufacturers and pilots? What rights did a passenger have? Was it necessary to get permission to fly over private property, etc.? The few law enforcement officers who did arrest the casual flyer for dangerous flying were usually embarrassed to find they had to turn him loose as there were no laws prohibiting his activities. These problems had to be resolved before commercial aviation could attract the capital it needed to grow and mature. One of the more challenging problems was State's rights versus the Federal Government. For instance, prior to Federal legislation, pilots

nautics Branch of the Department of Commerce. Compounding the problem was the fact, that while all recognized the need for rules, many feared overregulation.

Henry Ford, in spite of this unfavorable climate, was confident of the future of commercial aviation and realized, along with others, that both business and the general public had to be convinced of the reliability and safety of air transportation before real progress could be made. In 1925, he was ready to act on his beliefs and try to overcome the public's unfavorable perception by launching his own experimental and demonstration Air Transportation Service to carry company mail and freight between Ford Airport in Dearborn, Michigan and the Air Mail field at Maywood, Illinois (Chicago). This first flight, made on April 13, 1925, in the *Maiden Dearborn*, the second Stout Air Transport, was piloted by Edward Hamilton with Harry Russell as flight mechanic. Hamilton was one of the most experienced pilots available to Ford, having been a flight instructor for the Royal Canadian Air Force during the war, barnstorming afterwards and finally serving as a test pilot for Stout since 1922. Russell was also a fine pilot and both would eventually manage Ford Airport. The

the big plane return from its hazardous trip to Chicago.

In July, a second route to Cleveland, Ohio was established with the pilots again restricted to an overland flight. They were routed south to Toledo, Ohio and then east to Cleveland avoiding the shortcut across Lake Erie. The pilots were limited to flying round trips on alternate days as the stress of daily round trips was unknown and safety

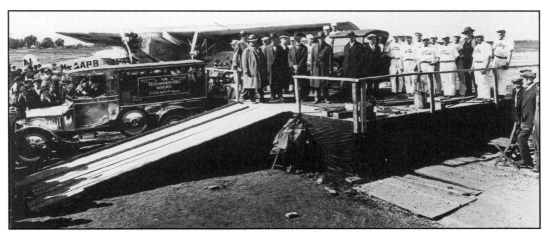

Inaugural flight of new route from Dearborn, Michigan to Buffalo, New York. The Ford plane carried all parts of a Model T car to be assembled on arrival by a crew of employees from the local Ford plant. (HFM 189.3747)

first flight carried 782 pounds of small automobile parts, 107 pounds of film and 116 pounds of company printed matter.[2] For safety reasons, the pilot was directed to follow the Indiana shoreline and avoid flying across Lake Michigan. So heightened was the interest and concern that something might happen to dash the public's expectations, that for nearly a week thereafter, Stout, Mayo, their associates and the inevitable reporters gathered each day at Ford Airport to watch

was a major concern. Quoting Mayo: *"Inasmuch as the venture is a new one with us and as the eyes of the whole world are centered on us, we are trying to use every precaution to make all our moves in the air a decided success."*

Ground was broken in Cleveland for a new Ford hangar in February 1926 and was occupied in June of the same year. All of Ford's aviation buildings as well as most of his automobile manufacturing buildings were designed by noted architect Albert Kahn. A Chicago area airfield was next on the list as Maywood Field in Chicago was under government control and was 25 miles north of the Ford factory in Hegeswisch, Illinois. Ford purchased 1,440 acres of farm land in nearby Lansing, Illinois overlapping into Munster, Indiana, establishing a private airfield and hangar that became operational in January 1927.[3] A small Verville bi-plane was purchased to run the U.S. Air Mail from Lansing, Illinois to the government airfield at Maywood, Illinois. Always looking to maximize assets and minimize expenses, Ford leased the outlying acres of the Lansing airfield back to the farmers for a share of their produce. In December 1930, the airport manager, complaining the market for corn was only 60 cents a bushel, requested approval to hold 2,000 bushels until after the first of the year for a better price.

So successful was Ford's air freight transportation experiment this first year, that in February 1926, Mayo was quoted in <u>Automotive Industries</u> (February 11,1926) to the effect that Ford was mapping out an air route between Detroit, New York, Boston and intermediate eastern cities. His enthusiasm outran practicality and, while none of these routes were ever attempted, his remarks did generate a great deal of publicity for Ford. Whether intentional or not, Ford was a master at making newsworthy proclamations that never came to pass. However, by 1927, he

had established another airfield next to his assembly plant in Hamilton, Ohio (just outside of Cincinnati) and in 1931, he had an airfield built to accommodate his wood product's facility at Iron Mountain in Michigan's Upper Peninsula.

Ford's air service was the first regularly scheduled air service in the United States dedicated to one company. It was also the first air service to actually run on schedule. When a plane took off, the time was duly noted as it roared over nearby Ford Headquarters and there were few acceptable excuses for being late. Although Mayo was quoted as saying they planned to start carrying paying passengers after six months, Ford Air Transportation Service was never utilized as a passenger carrier with the exception of a few company personnel being carried only with management approval. It was felt that a single engine plane was not satisfactory for passenger service and by the time they were building the Tri-Motor airplane, Bill Stout had established his own passenger service operating out of Ford Airport.

For his Air Transportation Service, Ford purchased the first five Stout Air Transport planes built at the new Stout factory in Dearborn provided by Ford. Naturally they were named *Maiden Dearborn I, II, III, IV, & V.* Having started with flights every other day with the first plane, Ford increased service to daily flights when the next Stout plane became available in April 1925. As more planes were built, service was extended from Dearborn to Cleveland in July 1925, and Dearborn to Buffalo in March 1927. To dramatize the convenience, versatility and practicality of air freight and help add drama to Ford's Air Transportation Service and the dedication of the new Cleveland Municipal Airport, Ford shipped all of the parts needed to build a Model T car on the first Cleveland flight. Seventeen employees from the local Ford assembly plant were on hand to unload the parts. They then assembled the car at the airport in one hour and three minutes after

spectator sport. A Cleveland to Buffalo run was added using local existing hangar facilities at Buffalo, but lasted only ten months. Here again, the transportation of parts for a Model T car and its assembly on arrival in Buffalo created desired publicity for Ford. To further help publicize Ford's aviation interests, specially built, highly polished Monel metal trucks marked *Air Transportation Service of Ford Motor Company,* provided service between the Ford factories and airports in Dearborn, Chicago, Cleveland and Buffalo. The Ford Air Transportation Service

Shortly after starting the Air Transprt Service, Ford introduced this Model T truck made of Monel metal to transport mail and freight between Ford plants and the airports in various cities. Monel metal kept its high luster while resisting corrosion. (HFM 833.43618)

the plane landed. A crowd, reported at over 200,000 was on hand to celebrate the dedication of the new airfield, the arrival of the Ford plane and the inauguration of the night air mail service between New York, Cleveland and Chicago. Aviation was definitely a

continued until August 1932, by which time Ford's experimental air service had demonstrated the reliability, safety and economic feasibility of air transportation and it was felt there were now sufficient commercial airlines available to service Ford's needs.

By the time Henry Ford terminated his Air Transportation Service, Ford planes had traveled almost two million miles, carrying nearly thirteen million pounds of freight and mail, with only two fatal accidents. They had completed 93% of their 10,149 scheduled flights, with only 58 cancellations due to mechanical problems, 30 of which were with the early single engine 2ATs in the first two years of operations.

Ford had publicly stated that they were operating an experimental air service to prove the feasibility of commercial aviation, and all operating and cost information obtained from his Air Transportation Service was freely shared. Based on their own experience, Ford's airplane catalogs of 1927 and 1928, devoted a great deal of space to suggestions on the organization and financing of an airline along with general information about the requirements of the typical landing field. Ford's ads continuously stressed their willingness to share all operating information.

Because of the closeness of the Ford/Stout aviation connection, many writers have confused the Ford Air Transportation Service and the Stout Air Services as being one and the same airline and, as a result, Ford has been credited with initiating uniforms for pilots and carrying the first flight attendants. Ford Air Transportation Service had no need for uniforms or flight attendants as they carried only company freight and mail and never carried paying passengers. It was Stout's airline, The Stout Air Services, a public passenger carrier, that started the practice of uniformed pilots and flight attendants.[4]

United States Air Mail Contract

As early as 1910, Congress had considered the possibilities of establishing an air mail service. Ironically, it wasn't until 1917, when the United States was at war and Congress started to appreciate aviation, that they granted the Post Office a budget to develop an air mail service. It was the intent of the Post Office to demonstrate the safety and reliability of aviation, by flying the mail themselves and eventually turning the system over to private contractors. While sufficient incentive would be provided the private contractor to make it financially attractive for them to fly the mail initially, the long term goal of the Post Office was to make the airmail pay for itself and that meant passenger service would have to be developed. Passenger service meant safety was paramount and safety started with the pilots. As there were no rules or regulations governing the qualifications of a pilot or a plane, the Air Mail Service set their own. To be considered, a pilot needed a minimum of 500 hours flying experience and, once hired, had to pass regular physical examinations. As important as the pilots, were the planes and ground operations with properly located and equipped airports and emergency fields staffed with qualified personnel. Planes, unlicensed at this time, were for the most part refurbished war surplus, open cockpit deHavilland DH4s, provided to the Post Office Department by the Army. Having to work with these war surplus planes, stringent safety procedures were set in place. Planes were inspected after every four or five hour trip according to a 180 point check list. Engines were overhauled every 100 hours and airframes every 750 hours. The wisdom of these procedures was born out in the statistics. During 1924, the last year the Post Office flew all the airmail routes, best estimates indicated itinerant flyers had one fatality for every 13,500 miles flown. The U.S. Air Mail Service pilots had one fatality for every 463,000 miles flown.

From its inauguration in 1918 through 1924, the Air Mail Service was comprised mainly of the transcontinental New York to San Francisco route and was mostly for show. Flying only in daytime, it was very expensive to use and maintain and saved little time over the railroads. It wasn't until 1925 that the Air Mail Service came into its own with the installation of aerial navigation beacons. Twenty four-inch revolving beacons of 7,500,000 candle power were installed every ten miles across the United States allowing the planes to fly at night. This enabled the delivery of mail from coast to coast, in a little over 30 hours versus the railroads' three day trip. By mid 1925, the delivery of air mail was deemed successful enough to turn it over to private contractors and to begin expanding the service to all major cities.

On September 21, 1925, the Postmaster General of the United States advertised for bids under the recently enacted Kelly Air Mail Act which provided for private contractors to carry the airmail. Henry Ford, who was fully committed to the development of commercial aviation, was operating the only daily scheduled air service in the United States. Ford had been working quietly behind the scenes to assure that he was awarded the Contract Air Mail (CAM-7) contract between Detroit and Chicago and his people had been visiting postal officials since early July to assure that they (the Post Office) *"have their*

Ford pilot Lawrence Fritz in typical flight gear. Fritz flew the first Contract Air Mail on a round trip between Dearborn, Michigan and Cleveland, Ohio on February 15, 1926. Like many early Ford pilots, Fritz rose to prominent aviation positions becoming an Air Force Major General in World War II and an American Airlines Vice President after the war. (Hudek 189.4082)

advertisement in line with what we can do."

Newspaper headlines in early September 1925, such as *"Ford Air Mail Bid Sure To Win"* and *"Ford Air Lines Soon To Carry Mail,"* months before the bids had even been advertised, forced the Postmaster General to characterize the reports as premature and stated that airmail contracts would be let in accordance with law. However, because of their concern for the success of the private airmail scheme, postal officials were extremely wary of inexperienced and financially weak groups winning bids, and they were certainly delighted that Ford was interested and would probably have done almost anything to assure the acceptance of his proposal.

Detroit's Postmaster Charles Kellogg announced on January 10, 1926 that Ford, who had won the mail contracts for Detroit to Cleveland (CAM 6) and Detroit to Chicago (CAM 7), would be the first private contractor to carry the mails starting February 1, in safe and suitable aircraft, six times a week. On January 12, Ford was advised these flights would be delayed until February 15, 1926 to allow Washington based postal officials to participate in the inaugural ceremonies.[5] Although Ford Airport was located in Dearborn, adjacent to Detroit, Dearborn was not in the Detroit Postal District and, therefore, not part of the Contract Air Mail route. The local Postmaster was not able to resolve this absurd situation until shortly before February

15 with the result that few First Flight envelopes bear the distinctive Dearborn First Flight cachet. When February 15 was over, it promised a rewarding future for commercial airmail and Ford with 249 pounds carried on both routes at $1.08 a pound. Unfortunately, most of the mail was from airmail postal cover collectors and, over the next twenty nine months, Ford's average flight would carry just over 10 pounds of mail and generate only $11 in revenues.

Early in 1925, Ford had offered to fly the airmail without compensation to help the Post Office develop data on which to base its rates and schedules. In 1926, they were arguing that their proposal to carry the mail should have been at the rate of 67.5% of total revenue instead of 6.75 ¢ an ounce quoted in their bid. They lost! Disagreements also arose over how much weight was actually carried during February 1926 and they exchanged lengthy letters over a two ounce (13¢) difference on CAM 6 and a four pound ($4.32) difference on CAM 7. Obviously, in light of the amount of money discussed, neither dispute was worth the time and effort to write the letters.

In March 1927, looking to expand their operations, the Post Office inquired if Ford was interested in the Detroit to Buffalo mail contract. Ford replied in the affirmative, but only with the guarantee of 150 pounds of mail daily. The Post Office never pursued the discussion.

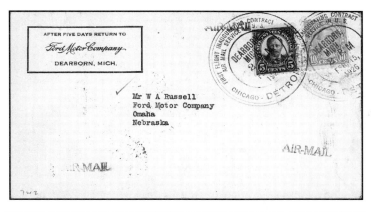

Airmail covers for the first Contract Air Mail flights flown by Ford on February 15, 1926. Top cover is CAM flight 6 (Detroit to Chicago) with distinctive DEARBORN cachet cancellation. Bottom cover is CAM flight 7 (Detroit to Cleveland) with distinctive DETROIT cachet cancellation. (O'Callaghan collection)

covering the additional costs of providing the administrative and security services required by the Post Office contract and the publicity value of being first with the mail had evaporated. On July 19, 1928, CAM 6 and 7 airmail contracts were terminated. Ford had pioneered another phase of aviation carrying over 32,000 pounds of air-mail.

Another of the early private contractors who started flying the U.S. Mail in April 1926, also used Ford planes. Four of the Stout Air Transports, now built under Ford ownership, were delivered in December 1925 to Florida Airways who had won the Miami to Jacksonville, Florida Contract Air Mail route (CAM 10).

Ford Motor Company advised the Post Office Department in May 1928 that National Air Transport (NAT), a new full service airline, would shortly be in a position to take over the CAM 6 route and that Ford would be terminating their mail contracts. Ford had maintained all along that he was operating a demonstration air service and that turning over the mail service to a permanent airline would be a logical step. In addition, it is probable that Ford was influenced by the fact that the meager mail revenues came nowhere near

Ford was not alone in his vision of the future of aviation. The potential of the Air Mail Act and the pending aviation regulations working their way through Congress lured William Rockefeller and others to invest in Colonial Air Lines, a forerunner of American Airlines and convinced Philip Wrigley, Charles Kettering and Marshall Field among others to form National Air Transportation

(NAT), a forerunner of United Airlines. Virtually all of these new air lines were formed solely to bid on the Contract Air Mail (CAM) routes as the subsidies in most cases guaranteed financial success.

The Post Office wanted financial stability of a carrier and the prospect of passenger service being developed to ultimately eliminate postal subsidies. This meant large corporations and, as the Post Office controlled who would fly the mail and where they would fly it, they forced some 23 small carriers to merge into five major airlines by 1932 (United, American, TWA, Eastern and Pan American), connecting most of the major population centers of the United States. Their goal of eliminating postal subsidies would not be realized until the 1950s.

The mail subsidies would prove to be the difference between profit and financial disaster for the vast majority of the airlines until 1936 with the arrival of the Douglas DC 3 with its greater range, speed, reduced operating costs and 21 passenger capacity. They could fly from New York to Los Angeles in 16 hours and according to C. R. Smith, president of American Airlines, it was the first plane to be able to make money by just carrying passengers.

Pilot Training at Ford Motor Company

To qualify as a pilot in 1910, under the rules adopted by the Federation Aeronautique International, an individual had to, among other accomplishments: (a) make two flights, each covering without touching the ground, a circuit not less than 3 miles in length; (b) complete an altitude test consisting in rising to a minimum of 150 feet above the starting point and landing safely. Those rules applied, of course, only to those who desired a license from the Federation.

Prior to the enactment of the Air Commerce Act in 1926, governing the qualifications of private and commercial pilots and aircraft mechanics, anyone could fly anything they could get off the ground, and itinerant barnstormers would continue to kill themselves in obsolete, worn out airplanes with all the attendant publicity.[6] Worse, the Hollywood aerial stunt men made big news when they crashed and headlines like that appearing in the January 30, 1926 edition of Liberty magazine only made it worse. Blaring: *"He Knows He Is Going To Be Killed,"* the Liberty article went on to state, *"One by one the stunt flyers of the screen world have met death."*

Henry Ford didn't want pilots killing themselves in Ford airplanes and was undoubtedly aware of the U.S. Air Mail Service's safety program and record. As all Ford pilots had to be qualified to carry the U.S. Mail, they all had well over 500 hours experience. In addition, Ford used his Air Transportation Service as a vehicle for training pilots and airplane mechanics for the new owners of his Tri-Motor planes. Many of these Ford trained pilots went on to become leaders in the aviation industry as it matured.

Stated in a 1927 Ford sales brochure, under *"How to Organize an Air Line"* is found: *"At this stage of aviation, it is necessary that the Ford Motor Company exercise extreme care in placing its planes."* Tri-Motor pilots were either men nominated by the buyer for training by Ford or a few pilots kept on the Ford payroll to be available to a new purchaser. Ford was concerned about his and his airplane's reputation and wanted qualified pilots flying Ford planes. In 1929, Ford advertised: *"Purchasers of planes are welcome to send their own men to the school for this special training, if they meet the requirements. But we must ask them to consider our decision of their fitness final. So important do we regard this provision, that we reserve the right to decline to deliver a Ford plane unless the pilot who will fly it meets with the approval of the officials of our training school. We are determined that Ford planes shall be safe and that they shall be flown safely, insofar as it is within our power to control."*

Another 1929 ad read: *"Pilots of Ford planes are given flying experience, examined and approved by our operations department before Ford planes, no matter who owns them, can be permitted to go out with them at the controls."*

A 1931 letter to a potential pilot spelled out Ford's requirements. By now, they included 700 hours prior flying time and stated that most successful applicants were ex-Army pilots who had trained on all types of planes. If a pre-flight check-out with the chief Ford pilot was satisfactory, they proceeded to spend about 30 hours flying for Ford's Air Transportation Service combined with working about a month in various departments of the airplane manufacturing plant to become familiar with the construction of the plane. Most early pilots had extensive mechanical knowledge of their aircraft as they needed to actually fix their own plane in an emergency. Later, an understanding of the mechanics of a plane, let the pilot accurately diagnose and describe problems for ground personnel.

Salary and wage information is skimpy, but the pay records, complete with observations, of three of the first pilots employed by Ford were found in the Ford Motor Company Industrial Archives.

<u>Comments on Pay Record</u>

Edward Hamilton

> From Stout Metal Airplane Company
> June 1, 1925 $500
> August 1, 1927 $550 Operations
>   Superintendent
> May 31, 1928   quit - Purchased Ford plane. First class man. Top executive.

Leroy Sherman Manning

> Former Army pilot
> Jun 1, 1925 $400
> Jul 1, 1928 $450

AVIATION
January 12, 1929

Ford-trained pilots for Ford planes

WE BELIEVE that safety is the foundation on which the success of commercial aviation must be built. In building the Ford tri-motored, all-metal transport monoplane, we give first consideration to safety in its design and structure. Speed, comfort, maneuverability, climb, general performance, efficiency—all these have their proper place and receive the consideration they deserve. But in our opinion none of them supersedes safety in importance.

Aviation has not reached the stage, admittedly, where the human element in flying can be ignored or even regarded with indifference. We make the Ford plane as self-reliant as possible. But we are the last who would claim that the Ford plane, of itself, assures safe flight. A thoroughly trained and competent pilot is essential. And he must be experienced on the particular type of plane he is to fly.

To provide such pilots to purchasers of Ford planes, we maintain a pilot's training school at the Ford Airport, at Dearborn. To be admitted to it a prospective pilot must have had several hundred hours of flying, must pass physical examinations which parallel those of the United States air services, and must satisfy officials of the company that he is qualified, by his character and judgment, to be responsible for the lives of his passengers and for the good name of the Ford plane.

Purchasers of planes are welcome to send their own men to the school for this special training, if they meet the requirements. But we must ask them to consider our decision of their fitness final.

So important do we regard this provision, that we reserve the right to decline to deliver a Ford plane unless the pilot who will fly it meets with the approval of the officials of our training school.

We are determined that Ford planes shall be safe and that they shall be flown safely, insofar as it is within our power to control. The Stout Metal Airplane Company, Division of Ford Motor Company, Dearborn, Michigan.

Photo by R. Raymond Martin

Save up to $10. Order at:
newyorker.com/go/savenow6

NYRJ4FS4A   NYRJ4FS4B

BUSINESS REPLY MAIL
FIRST-CLASS MAIL   PERMIT NO. 107   BOONE IA

POSTAGE WILL BE PAID BY ADDRESSEE

THE
NEW YORKER
PO BOX 37617
BOONE, IA 50037-2617

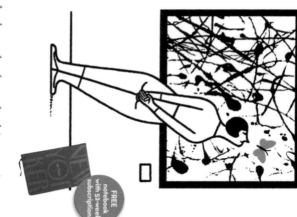

THE NEW YORKER

☐ **26 weeks for just $3.50 a week**
($91 total)

☐ **52 weeks for just $3.25 a week,
plus a FREE notebook!**
($169 total)

By subscribing, you agree to our user agreement
(condenast.com/user-agreement) and privacy policy and cookie statement
including your California rights (condenast.com/privacy-policy).

FREE
notebook
with 52-week
subscription!

Name _____ PLEASE PRINT

Address _____ Apt. _____

City _____ State ____ Zip _____

E-mail _____

Order online and SAVE UP TO $10.
Go to newyorker.com/go/savenow6

☐ Payment enclosed

A closer look at the bigger picture.
Save up to 60% off the cover price.

Dec 1, 1928 $500 In charge of
    operation & all test work
December 1, 1929 $580
July 1, 1930 $625
September 19, 1931 killed
Pay salary until Dec 31, 1931
(Flight mechanic, too.)

Lawrence Fritz

 From Aerial Surveys of Cleveland
August 1, 1925 $250-Assistant pilot
October 1, 1925 $300-Full fledged
    pilot
April 1, 1926 $325
October 1, 1926 $350
April 1, 1927 $375
July 30, 1927   Quit. Flew plane to
    Maddux Airlines in California and
    joined them. Would rehire.

By comparison, Carl Wentzel, a flight-test mechanic and one of the first employees transferred to the Airplane Division, was being paid $265 a month at the time of his death in the crash of a Ford plane in November 1930. The most complete record of any of Ford's aviation personnel was supplied by the daughter of Lycurgus Garriot. Hired by Ford in July 1916, he was trained as an aviation machinist by the Navy during World War I. Returning to Ford after the war, he was transferred to the Airplane Division as a mechanic in October 1925 at the rate of $1.00 an hour. In 1928 he was selected to go with Floyd Bennett and Bernt Balchen (Commander Richard Byrd's polar pilots) when they flew to Labrador to rescue the *Bremen* flyers who had crashed landed after being the first to cross the Atlantic Ocean from east to west. An *"unusually fine mechanic,"* he was promoted to foreman in January 1930 and then placed on a six month leave of absence to help maintain the Ford Tri-Motor airplanes purchased by the newly formed New York, Rio & Buenos Aires Airlines (later absorbed by Pan American Airways). Later in 1930, he participated in Ford's European trip demonstrating the Tri-Motor in most of the countries on the continent. At the time of his death in the crash of the Ford bomber in September 1931, he was earning $220 a month.

All of the glamour and excitement of aviation of the period focused on those who designed and those who flew the airplanes. It was a different story for those men in the factory. Ford was building his airplanes on an assembly line just as he did his cars and the same work rules applied. In a rare comment on life in Ford's airplane factory, Robert Baron, an inspector for the Airplane Division, relates in his diary the story of an aerial fatality at Ford Airport in 1927. *"He was on some trial flight prior to the reliability tour. He was killed within 150 feet of where I was working. No one was allowed to go out and help retrieve him from the plane. You had to stay on the job."* The pilot was Ralph Downs, flying a Woodson airplane and he became the first fatality at Ford Airport.

The first Ford Motor Company air fatality

and the first fatality under the new Contract Air Mail Service occurred on May 18, 1926 at Argo, Illinois (Chicago) when Ford pilot Ross Kirkpatrick crashed in the *Maiden Dearborn* while attempting to land in poor visibility caused by fog, smoke, haze and rain. This was the only fatal accident in a Ford operated Stout Air Transport, but it seemed to have crystallized Ford's thinking concerning his aviation policy as related by Charles Lindbergh at a later date:

> "• *Make monoplanes because they were simpler.*
> • *Make them out of metal because metal was the thing of the future.*
> • *Make them with more than one engine because they weren't going to have anymore forced landings.*"

Lindbergh commented that Ford had laid down three of the fundamentals that had formed the base of successful air transportation development and described this as *"an instance when his genius came out with exceptional clarity."*[7]

In eight years of manufacturing airplanes and operating the Air Transportation Service, Ford Motor Company compiled an excellent record with only five fatal accidents:

<u>Air Transportation Service:</u>
May 18, 1926, Ross Kirkpatrick in a 2AT
May 12, 1928, William Munn & Earl Parker in a 4AT

<u>Airplane Division:</u>
February 25, 1928, Harry Brooks in a Flivver
November 24, 1930, Myron Zeller & Carl Wentzel in a 5AT
September 19, 1931, Leroy Manning & Lycurgus Garriot in XB906

Notes - Chapter 3

(1)   Bulletin of <u>The Daniel Guggenheim Fund For the Promotion of Aeronautics #5</u> (March 10, 1928) *The Airplane and the British Empire* and #6 (May 22, 1928) *Aviation on the Continent. (page 32)*

(2)   The <u>New York Times</u> (April 19, 1925) reported: *"The company mail between those branches* (Chicago and Detroit) *averages 800 pounds, or 32,000 letters a day, each way. Each plane saves $1,250 a day in postage."* Considering the fact that only one plane was in operation and the report was released after only three days activity, this is an incredibly exaggerated statement. Just ten months later, Ford would carry a total of only 249 pounds of U.S. mail (about 8,000 letters), highly inflated by collectors covers, on four flights of the highly publicized inaugural United States Air Mail flights to and from Detroit and Chicago, and Detroit and Cleveland. *(page 35)*

(3)   The Lansing airport, sold in 1937, is still in use today. In May 1985, the hangar was placed on the <u>National Register of Historic Places</u>. *(page 36)*

(4)   Stanley Knauss, General Manager of the Stout Air Services related that to his knowledge they were the first to have uniformed pilots and stewards. It seems a natural thing to do: *"On any type of vehicle people rode on, a bus, streetcar, taxi, train or steamship, they all had uniformed personnel, it gave a sense of permanency. As far as the steward was concerned - it was a necessity. You couldn't just lock eight people in the cabin away from the pilot and let them alone. Flying was new and people became frightened or ill. They thought they should have someone aboard who could allay their fears and take care of them if they became ill or panicky."* (<u>Ford Archives Accession</u> 65, Box 32) *(page 38)*

(5)   Most writers have attributed the delay of the first air mail flight to the fact that the Stout Metal Airplane Factory burned to the ground January 17, 1926, but the announcement of the delay was made five days earlier on January 12, 1926. *(page 40)*

(6)   The Air Commerce regulations, promulgated December 31, 1926 were to be effective July 1, 1927. However, by the end of 1927, no airport had been certified. Only 110 pilots out of 1,800 applications, 100 mechanics out of 1,600 applicants and 140 airplanes out of 1,100 had been licensed or certified. Lindbergh's flight only compounded an already impossible deadline. Also, while the Air Commerce regulations required a pilot to have 200 hours in the air in order to qualify for a transport pilot's license, it did not, unfortunately, specify the type of aircraft in which the 200 hours of experience was to be gained. It could be Ford's little Flivver or his big Tri-Motor. *(page 42)*

(7)   This quote, and many of the others in this book attributed to Lindbergh, was contained in a letter dated November 13, 1959 to Frank Hill. Hill, co-author of <u>Ford: Expansion and Challenge 1915 - 1933</u> published in 1957, had interviewed Lindbergh extensively for his recollections of his association with Henry Ford. (<u>Ford Archives, Accession</u> 940, Box 27). *(page 46)*

4

STOUT METAL AIRPLANE COMPANY

Purchase

Once Henry Ford became interested in an idea, things moved fast. By late 1924, Stout's new factory was completed and finishing touches were being put on the airfield as the first plane landed in November. The airport was dedicated in January 1925 and in April, Ford announced the formation of his new Air Transportation Service. The airport terminal was also occupied in April and the construction of the dirigible mooring mast was underway. On August 1, 1925 Henry Ford announced the surprising purchase of the Stout Metal Airplane Company.

As late as March 20, 1925, <u>The New York Times</u> had quoted Edsel Ford as saying: *"it is not our purpose to enter the manufacturing field in aviation."* However, Henry Ford had already decided that if Stout's airplane company was going to amount to anything, it needed a large amount of capital and that he was the one to provide it. Within days of the first flight of the Ford Air Transportation Service flight to Chicago on April 13th, reports, that were denied, were circulating that Ford had made an offer to buy up all interests in the Stout Metal Airplane Company.

In fact, Stout had advised one of his investors, Edward Budd of the Budd Manufacturing Co., on April 10,1925, that Edsel Ford *"wants to take over the manufacturing end of this work at once,"* and *"is willing to pay $2000 for every $1000 put in."* During the Stout Metal Airplane stockholders meeting on April 14th, Stout reminded them that they had originally joined the venture to make Detroit the aviation center of the United States. He appealed to them to approve the offer and exchange their Stout Metal Airplane Company stock for stock in his newly formed Stout Air Services, a scheduled passenger air service: *"in order that your identity in aviation may not be lost for the mere making of a profit on your investment."*

Henry Ford, still smarting from several minority stockholders that had held up his purchase of the Detroit Toledo & Ironton (DT&I) railroad in 1920 and the Dodge Brothers minority stockholders suit in 1917, had told Stout that he would buy the company only if he got 100% of the stock. The stockholders had invested in Detroit aviation and several, perceiving Ford to be taking advantage of

Stout, were reluctant to see him grab Stout's company. Bill Stout later claimed: *"I had twice the job to unsell the stock as I ever did to sell it."* Stout prevailed however and on August 1, 1925, it was announced that Ford Motor Company had purchased all assets and stock of the Stout Metal Airplane Company. Ford had paid the general stockholders $2 for each $1 invested with Bill Stout and his working associates getting slightly more. The Stout Metal Airplane Company became a division of the Ford Motor Company for $1,300,000 and Bill Stout and key employees, Stanley Knauss, George Goin and Alex Runkis were placed in charge of aircraft manufacturing. Bill Stout requested that Ford have all Stout Metal Airplane Co. stock transferred through him (Stout), which would give him a final opportunity to persuade the original investors to reinvest their money in his new Stout Air Services company, formed to start a scheduled passenger airline service between Dearborn, Michigan and Grand Rapids, Michigan. Stout Metal Airplane Company records indicate 63 of the original investors reinvested in Stout Air Services.

On the announcement of the purchase, the New York Post (August 7, 1925) quoted Henry Ford: *"The first thing that must be done with aerial navigation, is to make it fool-proof. Just now its 90 percent man and 10 percent plane. That percentage must be turned around. We are not going into the racing business. What the Ford Motor Company means to do is to prove whether commercial flying can be done safely and profitably."*

What did the announcement of purchase mean to the public? Colonel William Mitchell, chief of all U.S. military aviation in World War I and most recently the former Assistant Army Air Chief, was quoted by the Detroit News (August 13, 1925) as declaring: *"Ford Motor Company's entrance into the field of aeronautics is the greatest incentive to commercial aviation in the history of flying."* In a later communication, Mitchell wrote Ford: *"The handling of aeronautics by the Federal Government is mere mockery. It has become a political football."* and *"I believe that the best hope in this country in the future* (for aviation) *is your organization."*

A New York Times story (November 14, 1926) stated: *"It took the entry of the Fords into the business of building and using airplanes to win the recognition of the air transport by the Government and engage even the present half-hearted support of the American people."*

Granting the impact of Ford's contribution, the laudatory comments were a bit overdone considering all the people involved and their hard work that had been expended to develop the rules and regulations that would be necessary to gain the public's confidence and allow commercial operators to buy and economically operate Ford planes. But such was the power of the Ford name.

Airplanes

A brief summary of who built what will make the following segment more understandable.

William Stout, as owner of the Stout Metal Airplane Company designed and built the following planes:[1]

AS-1   Air Sedan
        all metal 4 passenger

AP-1   Air Pullman
        all metal 8 person
        (named *Maiden Detroit*
        and later referred to as
        2AT-1 — sold to the
        Post Office)

2AT-2 thru 5 Air Transport
        all-metal 8 person (sold
        to Ford and named
        *Maiden Dearborn I, II,
        III & IV*)

William Stout as the manager of the Stout Metal Airplane Company, Division of Ford Motor Company, designed and built the following planes:

2AT- 6 thru 11 Air Transport
        all metal 8 person

3AT   Air Transport
        all metal three engines

Ford engineers of the Stout Metal Airplane Company, Division of Ford Motor Company, designed and built the following planes:[2]

4AT   Air Transport
        all metal three engines,
        12 passenger

5AT   Air Transport
        all metal three engines,
        14 passenger

Stout Air Transport (2AT)

While Bill Stout was building his all metal Air Sedan and Air Pullman using, out of necessity, war surplus aircraft engines, the planes themselves were designed for commercial use. Commenting on Stout's new Air Pullman, the British magazine <u>Flight</u>, (October 16, 1924) observed that Stout had bro-

Stout's first Air Pullman *Maiden Detroit* with Stout Metal Airplane Company management. Left to right are: Bill Stout, Stanley Knauss, general manager, Glen Hoppin, business manager, George Prudden, designer and Walter Lees, test pilot. (Hudek 1008.AP.2027)

Ford pilot Leroy Manning entering the cockpit by climbing up side of plane. As these planes were used by Ford to haul freight there was no other entrance to the cockpit. Although there was no legal requirement, all Ford pilots wore parachutes. (Hudek 1008.x.4.a)

sign was safe and profitable commercial air transportion, or as he was often quoted: *"A plane that could support itself in the air financially as well as physically."* The Air Pullman, later designated an Air Transport or 2AT, was first flown in February 1924 by veteran pilot Walter Lees. It had a cruising speed of 100 mph and a range of approximately 500 miles. It was equipped with a toilet and washroom and an electric self starter, although later models would not have these features.

ken from the pack by making no attempt to follow military design or to build from old war-stock material for the sake of economy as most aircraft manufacturers of the period were doing. The main object of Stout's de-

The Air Transport was designed to carry six people or 1,500 pounds of freight, plus a pilot and co-pilot, and was built with an eye towards capturing some of the Post Office's

Ford Air Transportion Service airplane and Monel metal Model T truck on display at the Michigan State Fair, September 1925. (Hudek 189.3004)

Showroom of the John Wanamaker Department Store in New York City featured the first airplane sold by Ford Motor Company. This plane was later purchased by Stout for his new Stout Air Services airline. (Hudek 1008.AP.2177.a)

airmail business, which at the time was using the war surplus deHavilland bi-planes. Nearly 5,000 of these planes, designed by Great Britain, had been built in the United States during the war with only 800 being shipped to Europe. They were powered by the same 400 hp Liberty engines as Stout's Air Transport, and while the engine and plane had been modified for better performance, they only had a 500 pound freight capacity. But selling the Stout Air Transport was an uphill fight. The airmail pilots were comfortable with their deHavillands due to their surplus power and maneuverability and they were reluctant to change to the larger, less agile 2AT. In addition, the cockpit on the 2AT was located in front of the wing. Although it was for better visibility, the veteran airmail

pilots felt that their being in front of the wing just put them closer to danger in case of a crash. In addition, the newly formed private air services were not interested in carrying passengers, but only the airmail for the government subsidy, and viewed the size and price of $25,000 for the 2AT as excessive for their needs.

The first 2AT, the *Maiden Detroit*, was designed for a pilot and co-pilot, but when sold to the Post Office it was changed to a single seat as only one pilot was used and visibility was not as good for a single pilot with a double seat configuration. This first plane was also built with a full celluloid windshield and quick opening side windows. Future 2ATs would be built as both single and dual seat planes depending on whether they would be used for freight or passenger service, and had only small frontal windscreens. In addition there was a partial cover over the cockpit area for aerodynamic purposes, but hinged at the rear for ease of access and quick departure in case of an emergency. The 2ATs, used by Ford for freight operations, were entered by the pilot climbing up the side of the plane to the cockpit using toe holes built into the side of the fuselage. However, as the planes used by Wanamaker and Florida Airways were for passenger service, the pilots entered these planes through the passenger cabin. The second 2AT which was the first built at the new Stout factory at Ford Airport in Dearborn was christened *Maiden Dearborn* but later re-named *Maiden Dearborn I* when the second ship was placed in Ford service, and christened *Maiden Dearborn II*. Ford purchased this first plane for his newly created Air Transportation Service for $22,500. After Ford decided to start his own air service, he arranged to purchase twenty of the surplus Liberty engines he had originally produced during the war, from the government, for $2,000 each. He then purchased the next three 2ATs from Stout for $20,000 each and had his own engines installed. Stout's cost on these planes was estimated at $15,000.

The first commercial sale of a Ford plane, and the seventh 2AT built, was to the John Wanamaker Company of New York City in October 1925 for $23,000. The four seats and the cabin walls were upholstered in blue leather by men from the Lincoln Division. Henry Ford sent a personal note to Rodman Wanamaker when the plane was delivered: *"We take great pleasure in knowing that the first Ford-built airplane to be delivered to a customer is going to John Wanamaker. Having in mind that the first Ford car delivered in the New York District went to your company."* (In 1904, John Wanamaker Co. had become the first authorized Ford dealer in New York City.)

The plane was publicly displayed at the First National Motor Bus show held in Convention Hall in New York City and the International Air Races at Mitchell Field, Long Island. It was then offered for sale in Wanamaker's New York store for $25,000. Just three months later, on January 5, 1926, the plane was removed from their store and purchased by the Stout Air Services for their new Detroit to Grand Rapids route.

The last four 2ATs were sold in December 1925 to Florida Airways for $22,500 each. Florida Airways, a newly formed airline whose co-founders included World War I ace Eddie Rickenbacker, had William Mayo on the Board of Directors and had received a $25,000 investment from Stout Air Services. Unfortunately, it ceased operations in December 1926 with one of the 2AT planes having been destroyed in a hurricane, two purchased by Stout Air Services and one reacquired by Ford Motor Co.

Although many in aviation were against Federal regulations, the Air Commerce Act of 1926 was signed into law May 20th, creating the Aeronautics Branch[3] of the Department of Commerce to administer the enumerated duties and responsibilities. One of the chief provisions was the Regulatory Powers which provided for the Licensing and Operation of Aircraft, the Licensing of Pilots and Mechanics and the establishment of Air Traffic Rules. As a result, all of the single

to Florida Airways. The following day another article was headed *"Three Tin Geese in Wreck, Nashville."*

Stout Tri-Motor (3AT)

While the Post Office was happy with Ford's involvement in the Contract Air Mail routes, Colonel Paul Henderson, in charge of the U.S. Air Mail Service, was still very concerned with the safety and freight capacity

The last four single-engine airplanes built by Ford were sold to the newly formed Florida Airways who had won one of the Post Office Contract Air Mail routes. (Hudek 833.45075)

engine 2AT aircraft were grounded July 20, 1928 as it was not feasible to meet the new aircraft licensing requirements - specifically: structural weakness in the wings of the 2AT. This in spite of the fact one plane had flown over 132,000 miles and collectively they had just one fatality, and that was weather-related.

The earliest documented use of the nickname Tin Goose was in connection with this single engine Ford plane, not the famous Tri-Motor that followed. A December 30, 1925 headline in a Monroe, Michigan newspaper read: *"One of Henry's Tin Geese is storm victim"* referring to one of the four planes delivered

of available planes. He was especially concerned about night flying and the fog shrouded mountainous areas such as that near Bellefonte, Pennsylvania where several airmail pilots had been lost. To illustrate the primitive status of aviation at the time, consider several of the U.S. Air Mail Service rules and instructions of the early 1920s:

• Don't take the machine into the air unless you are satisfied it will fly.

• Never leave the ground with the motor leaking.

• Never get out of the machine with the engine running.

• Do not trust altitude instruments.

• No machine must taxi faster than a man can walk.

• Pilots should carry hankies in a handy position to wipe goggles off.

• If you see another machine near you, get out of the way.

Colonel Henderson liked Stout's all-metal *Maiden Detroit* but thought it somewhat under-powered and had provided a 500 hp Packard engine to be installed for testing purposes. This was only a stop gap measure however, as Henderson and his people continued to express their belief that a three motored plane was the only safe answer. Mayo, referring to Henderson's concerns, had written Edsel Ford in June 1925, that: *"this fits right in with the thought we had on the most safe type of passenger plane - - - and I think it is well for us to develop this plane as quickly as possible."*

During this period, there was a proliferation of airplane manufacturers, suppliers and flying organizations and most of the manufacturers built one or two planes before disappearing. By 1929, in the Detroit area alone, there were twelve airplane manufacturers, six airplane engine manufacturers and twenty-eight aircraft parts and supply companies. In addition, there were eleven flying services, nine flying schools and a dozen aeronautical clubs and organizations. Most of the airplane companies designed planes for the military which offered the largest sales potential and little thought was given to the almost non-existent commercial market. Ford was convinced by now that the future of commercial aviation lay in larger multi-engine ships for economy of size and safety. The Fords could afford the luxury of believing, and acting on their beliefs, that they should develop planes for the commercial market with the military adapting the Ford planes to their use. The Literary Digest (August 1926) quoted Ford *"We hope to produce a plane that will be so cheap as to make air service profitable without government aid,"* as opposed to the heavy

The first Ford Tri-Motor model 3AT. It was Bill Stout's attempt to design a large three-motor plane for Henry Ford. Stout modified one of his 2ATs and it flew like it looked, having to be landed under full power. It was destroyed when a mysterious fire demolished Stout's factory in January 1926. Note open cockpit on top of plane. (Hudek 189.3172)

The Stout Metal Airplane Company factory after January 1926 fire. There was much speculation about the cause of the fire but it did rid Henry Ford of the despised 3AT airplane. (HFM 883.45237)

Another view of the Stout Metal Airplane Company showing the total devastation wrought by the fire. (HFM 883.45385)

subsidies given commercial aviation in Europe.

The single largest road block to building larger planes had been the availability of a light weight, high performance motor of unquestioned reliability or as air pioneer Louis Bleriot had remarked: *"engine perfection must be developed to the point where they stop only at the wish of the pilot!"*[4] The Navy, now committed to aircraft carriers in the fleet, demanded light weight as well as reliability in their new engines. As a result, the Navy had subsized the development of the new air-cooled 200 hp Wright J-4 Whirlwind engine which fully met both of these needs. Introduced to the civilian market in late 1924, it was quickly recognized as the answer to designing larger aircraft, and Ford had Stout develop plans for a three-engine plane. By

November 1925, Stout had modified the structure of one of the single engine 2ATs by widening the center wing section by ten feet, strengthening the fuselage and landing gear and burying two of the new Wright radial engines in the wings and one in the nose. The open cockpit was located on top of and just in front of the wing. Designated a 3AT, it was ugly and an aerodynamic disaster.

Major Schroeder conducted the first test flight on November 24, 1925 and refused to take the plane up for further tests. It handled poorly in the air and it was necessary to land under full power. It is reported that Schroeder had in fact stated during construction that burying the engines in the wings was not practical, citing the poor experience of German companies. Henry Ford, who had high hopes for this plane, directed Larry Fritz, another Ford pilot, to test the plane. Same results! The Herald American, (Syracuse, New York, December 20,1925) reported: *"The big machine will not carry the load expected of it, nor climb as rapidly and land at as slow a speed as it should."* Ford was furious. He had a failure on his hands. On January 17, 1926, the airplane factory with the 3AT inside, mysteriously burned to the ground. Unbelievably, eight days later on January 25th, Stout had a proposal ready to build another three-engine plane almost identical to the hated 3AT.

It was shortly after the fire that Henry Ford was quoted as saying: *"that for the first time*

in my life I have bought a lemon, and I don't want the world to know about it," and Bill Stout was sent off on an extended public relations tour. There was never an official explanation of the fire, but many people connected with the airplane operations at the time, felt certain that Henry Ford gave orders to get rid of the plane (but not necessarily the building.)[5] Aiding this speculation was an article in the Detroit News (January 18, 1926) commenting: *"Yesterday's fire is the first serious one the Ford Motor Company has suffered in its Detroit plants."* It was the only one in 22 years. The News story went on: *"Seemingly undisturbed by the $500,000 fire of unknown origin — Henry Ford talked only of his plans for the future,"* and headlined the story, *"New Ford Air Plant To Rise On Ruins."* In his Oral Reminiscence[6] for Ford's 50th anniversary in 1953, Stout related a comment Henry Ford made at the time of the fire: *"Stout, don't look so sad. It is the best thing that ever happened to you. It is such an advantage that I wouldn't be surprised if you set it yourself,"* and laughed. *"Now we can build the type of building and hangar that we should have built in the first place."*

A memo dated January 19, 1926, directed that the loss be stated to the Dearborn Fire Department as $71,515.48 for the building and $404,892.76 for the contents. Total insurance coverage was listed as $39,000. A company memo dated December 30, 1930 lists the following planes that were destroyed in the fire:

No 1 Mail Plane (2AT-1, the former *Maiden Detroit*), three Liberty airplanes (2ATs) in process at the time of the fire, and the 3AT. Newspaper reports state the losses included a new $10,000 Packard 500 hp engine and 13 of the scarce, new Wright J-4 engines valued at $4,500 each. The loss of the new Wright engines was a blow. The Navy having subsidized their development, had priority on production which severely limited engines available for commercial use. Only 125 had been delivered to the commercial market by the end of 1925.

chusetts Institute of Technology and New York University, offering degrees in Aeronautical Engineering. Later, Ford would participate with the University of Detroit in offering students a work-study program leading to a degree in Aeronautical Engineering.

First of the new breed of Ford Tri-Motors - 4AT-1. Built by Ford engineers in the new Ford Engineering building in just five months after the fire. First few units had open cockpits, tail skids and half-moon windows similar to the 2AT. All were rebuilt later to more modern standards. (Hudek 189.3435)

ued at $4,500 each. The loss of the new Wright engines was a blow. The Navy having subsidized their development, had priority on production which severely limited engines available for commercial use. Only 125 had been delivered to the commercial market by the end of 1925.

While considering the failure of the 3AT, it must be kept in mind that aircraft design was in its infancy. The University of Michigan had been the first to offer a degree in Aeronautical Engineering in 1916 and by 1922 there were still only five schools in the United States who even offered aeronautical courses much less a degree. As late as January 1926, there were only two other schools, Massa-

Ford Tri-Motor (4AT & 5AT)

On April 13, 1926 Ford announced that *"Planes manufactured from now on will be of the multi-motored type with three air-cooled engines."* This announcement must be considered in the context of the times to appreciate its full impact. In 1926, only six of 28 American commercial plane manufacturers were listed as building an aircraft with more than one engine, five of which were one of a kind experimental models. In reality, the only one available for purchase was Fokker's F VIIa-3m, made of a fabric covered metal fuselage and plywood covered wings. Fokker had added two engines to his successful single engine F VIIa to take ad-

AVIATION
October 19, 1928

POWER POWER POWER

CUT ANY ENGINE ON A FORD PLANE AND YOU STILL HAVE PLENTY OF POWER

PILOTS undergoing training on Ford Tri-motors at the Ford Airport at Dearborn soon learn what it means to have a plane that will carry on with a dead engine.

For their course includes the cutting of any engine, by the chief pilot, in a steep climb, in a sharply banked turn. They learn from actual experience that there is no time when a Ford plane can't be brought to horizontal flight when an engine suddenly dies.

Another thing about this power. With three engines working the power load with the 5-AT is 10.6 pounds. There's the power to pull you out of a small field—to climb quickly over obstructions. It helps the pilot out of those slight mistakes in judgment where only a world of power will carry the plane through safely. Even with only two engines you have more power for your load than many a plane possesses. The power load then is only 15.9. Still plenty of margin, plenty of reserve.

More than half the accidents in commercial aviation, according to the Department of Commerce, are attributable to the pilot. But how often is the real reason the fact the plane wouldn't come through as the pilot expected, because the sheer, brute power he needed wasn't available?

In the Ford Tri-motor there's all the power you need or want. Even with one engine dead. Safe flying starts with power—dependable, uninterrupted power and plenty of it. The Stout Metal Airplane Company, Division of Ford Motor Company, Dearborn, Michigan.

FORD TRI-MOTOR
5-AT

Span 77 ft. 10 ins. Maximum speed, 133 M.P.H. Maximum radius of action (standard equipped) 5 to 6 hours. Ceiling, 18,000 ft. Weight empty, 7500 lbs. Disposable load, 6000 lbs. Power load, 3 engines, 10.6 lbs. per H.P.; 2 engines, 15.9. Cabin accommodates 14 passengers, pilot and mechanic. Construction: ALL-METAL *throughout, exposed surfaces Alclad alloy. Power: 3 Pratt & Whitney Wasps, totaling 1275 H.P. Price, complete with standard equipment including instruments, seats, toilet, etc., fly-away Dearborn, $55,000. (Prices and specifications subject to change without notice.)*

Early Ford planes, as was common on many airlines, featured wicker passenger chairs. Seat belts were an option. (Hudek 0.1250)

Dearborn to the delight of Henry and Edsel Ford and a few Ford executives. With the fiasco of the 3AT fresh in mind, attendance was restricted as Henry Ford wanted to make sure this plane wouldn't also embarrass them. After rave reviews by Schroeder of his morning tests, the plane was jubilantly demonstrated before the press and executives of several of the budding airline companies.

In a July press release, Ford emphasized one of Stout's ideas: *"The outstanding feature of the plane, and one which has a big safety element, is the extreme vision afforded the pilot and mechanic, who sit in front of the cabin in advance of the wing, which allows*

vantage of the exposure afforded by the first National Air Tour held in September 1925. But Fokker continued to make other single engine planes as well as his new tri-motor. Ford's decision to concentrate on only a three-engine aircraft was quite farsighted given the prevailing concepts and opinions.

Following the destruction of Stout's factory in January 1926, development and construction of this new three-engine airplane was moved to a portion of the Engineering Laboratory building while a new factory was being built.

On the morning of June 11, 1926, the new three-engine airplane (4AT), designed and developed by Ford engineers only five months after the fire, was test flown. For fifty minutes Major Schroeder and flight mechanic Harry Russell roamed the skies over

Cockpit of early 4AT model. Only the most rudimentary gauges were used. Several other gauges were mounted on the outboard engine struts. The large bar with knob between the steering wheels is the Johnson bar brake lever and, contrary to popular belief, it was the only major automobile part used in the Ford plane. (Hudek 189.4101)

First Tri-Motor built for the Canadian Government (6AT-1) being lowered into the Rouge River at the Ford plant. It was the larger 5AT airframe utilizing the more economical Wright J6 engines that were standard on the 4AT model. (HFM 833.53178)

Wing of a Ford Tri-Motor being used as a review stand at Selfridge Field, Mt. Clemens, Michigan. A demonstration of the strength of the nearly three foot thick wings. (HFM 189.3725)

This first 4AT model, while a great success, would undergo many refinements in the next several years resulting in the 5AT, which, while looking very similar to the 4AT, was really quite different. The first few planes had an open cockpit, thanks to Major Schroeder's insistence, a tail skid and no brakes. An open cockpit was considered essential by most pilots of the era so that they could feel the wind on their face, hear the sound of the wind in the guy wires and get out quickly with a parachute in an emergency. These first few early Ford planes were later rebuilt with closed cockpits, brakes and tail wheels. They were powered by three of the new Wright J-4 engines of 200 hp each and accommodated 12 passengers. In July 1928, the 5AT was introduced. It was a larger model with more powerful engines, some of which generated a total of over 1200 hp vs. the total 600 hp in the first 4AT model. The 5AT was faster, had a larger wing span and 14 passenger capacity and proved to be the most successful and popular passenger plane in the United States over the next few years. It was used by virtually all airlines of the U.S. and Latin

each of them to see in every direction on both sides of the plane. It is said to be the first time the vision problem has really been solved in a big plane - the most serious problem of all in the construction of large airplanes."

America. The other models, 6AT, 7AT, 8AT, 9AT, 11AT and 13AT, were modified 4AT and 5AT airframes with different engine combinations.

Because of the lack of color photography, most people have assumed the Tri-Motor airplanes were all the natural aluminum color with one or two exceptions. In fact, the big Ford planes were very colorful. Factory work orders covering exterior colors have been found for 95 of the planes, mostly 5AT models, covering three shades of green, four shades of blue, two shades of gold and red, brown, silver and several burnished or highly polished show jobs.

Airline Use

Just as Ford was introducing his new Tri-Motor passenger plane the Travelers Insurance Company of Hartford, Connecticut, in late 1926, removed policy restrictions on the use of aircraft for transportation: *"when using licensed planes operated by licensed pilots on regular passenger routes between certified airports."* (Automotive Industries December 9, 1926) Their surveys showed *"that there was little greater risk than normally beset pedestrians and users of automobiles."* Insurance was still expensive though. One underwriter offered a regular $100,000 death or injury policy for a $400 premium. Including an air mishaps rider jacked the premium to $4,000. By mid 1927, however, it was possible to insure ten passengers in a Ford

Tri-Motor for $10,000 each for a nominal annual premium of $1,500.

In July 1929, the Transcontinental Air Transport (TAT) and the Pennsylvania and Santa Fe Railroads combined to offer *"Coast To Coast, Two days by plane - Two nights by train"* service. Passengers would leave New York City in the evening by train and switch back and forth, traveling by Ford Tri-Motor during the day and trains by night, finally arriving at Los Angeles airport in the afternoon. As an indication of the Ford Tri-Motor's reputation at the time, the technical committee of TAT, headed by Charles Lindbergh and including the now retired Major Thomas Lanphier, selected and ordered 11 Ford Tri-Motors, because as their literature stated: *"Over a period of years, operating through the four seasons and daily schedule service, Ford planes have compiled a record of millions of miles of safe, comfortable, 'on time' flight that may well be compared with the records of our greatest railroads."* It was reported that Lindbergh felt so strongly about using Ford planes that he threatened to resign his position when senior management tried to insist on the use of other aircraft.

Other major customers for new Ford Tri-Motor airplanes were:

Army, Navy & Marines	22
Maddux Air Line (TWA)	16
National Air Transport (United)	11
Southwest Air Fast Express	

(American)	10
Pan American	9
Stout Air Services (United)	8

(Airlines later absorbed by those in parenthesis)

In addition, multiple plane orders were received from Robertson Aircraft Corp., Curtiss Flying Service, Northwest Airways, Cia Mexicana de Aviacion, Colonial Air Transport, Pacific Air Transport and others. While most airlines thought the Ford name on the tail of the Tri-Motor added a degree of respectability, Colonel Louis Brittin, one of the prime movers of Northwest Airways, is reported to have ordered the Ford name taken off the tail remarking: *"Ford doesn't own them anymore."* This in spite of the fact that Mayo and Stout served on his Board of Directors. Most other major airlines, ended up with Ford Tri-Motor in service through their acquisition of smaller lines. It is estimated that more than 100 airplanes around the world used Ford Tri-Motor airplanes. The National Air and Space Administration brochure Progress in Aircraft Design since 1903, published in 1976, states the Ford Tri-Motors: *"formed the backbone of the scheduled airline industry in the late 1920s and 1930s."*

The Ford airplane sales department consisted mainly of Bill Mayo, whose many aviation connections and the massive Ford aviation advertising program generated most leads. Initially, Mayo envisioned the Ford dealer network selling the small personal planes they were planning with the factory handling the large planes and commercial accounts. The small plane never developed and Mayo continued as the chief salesman although he was later assisted by several outside salesmen.

Airplane Development

In 1926, observing how the tail skids on planes were tearing up the airport sod, Ford engineers Charles Smith and Harold Hicks developed and patented the first airplane tail wheel. This and the use of concrete runways led to brakes on planes which previously were slowed by the friction of the tail skid. Ford Tri-Motor 4A-11, built in October 1927, was the first Ford plane equipped with a tail wheel. Most Ford pilots refused to test the plane, fearing they would lose control in landing. Interestingly, Ford pilot Leroy Manning reported that in his 1929 visit to Germany, when workers rushed out to help turn his plane around as was their normal task, they were amazed when he locked one wheel, gunned the engine and swung the plane around in its own length.

Safety as we know it today didn't exist in the 1920s. Parachutes were not required and seat belts were not mandated until 1930. The specifications on the order for 4AT-6 from the Standard Oil Company in March 1927 included: *"The Cabin floor to be provided with rings, to which chairs may be secured when in flight."* In addition, period photo-

© P & A photos

Adaptability of the
Ford tri-motored, all-metal transport

THE Ford tri-motored transport monoplane is adaptable to almost any special requirement an air-line operator may have.

It may be used as a seaplane, with twin floats. It can be equipped with skis for work in snow and ice. For work from fields in high altitudes it is equipped to meet these conditions.

It can be used for passengers exclusively—or passengers, express and mail. Its capacity is great enough to permit carrying sufficient passengers on short trips to make the work profitable. On the other hand, if the run is a long one, it can carry sufficient fuel for a non-stop flight, and still leave ample space and lift for carrying pay loads.

In short, whatever the route, the location, the type of work an operator is carrying on or contemplating, he will find a study of the capabilities of the Ford tri-motored, all-metal transport monoplane — as applied to his own work — useful to him in forming and carrying out his plans.

We will be glad to consult and advise with air-line operators. This service is rendered without cost or obligation to those requesting it. Communicate direct with

THE STOUT METAL AIRPLANE COMPANY
Division of
FORD MOTOR COMPANY
Dearborn, Michigan

THANK YOU *for mentioning* AVIATION

graphs show people standing in front of airplanes with running propellers. All would learn by experience.

By 1930, Ford held or had applied for 35 aviation related patents, including brakes, tail wheels, stabilizers, shock absorbers, wing mail bins, wing lights, radio beacons and airplane superchargers. Ford, remembering his trials and tribulations over the Selden patent, levied no fee on others for use of his patents, stating: *"Patents are silly things when they are used to hinder any industry. We take patents on our own developments or discoveries only to prevent others from freezing us out when they may chance to make the same discovery."*

Ford <u>Accounting Instructions</u>, in June 1925, had directed that Ford planes be depreciated 20% a year and that engines be written off in 500 hours. In March 1930, depreciation was increased to 24% a year on the plane, but engine life was extended to 2,000 hours (200,000 miles). While accounting was setting high depreciation rates on the planes, a 1930 sales brochure proclaimed *"No Ford Plane Has Ever Worn Out,"* and indeed, a Ford Motor Company

Ford 5AT-69, equipped with floats by TWA in order to operate from Downtown Skyport in lower Manhattan in New York City. (Hudek)

Ford 5AT-73, one of the later Ford Tri-Motor planes. While similar to the model 4AT, the model 5AT was larger and proved to be the airplane of choice for most airlines of the day. The NACA engine cowlings and wheel spats were designed to reduce drag. (Hudek)

Northwest Airways 5AT-48 Ford Tri-Motor. Colonel Britten, head of Northwest, was reported to have had the Ford name removed from the tail saying: *"Ford doesn't own them anymore."* (Hudek)

survey in 1945 found 90 Tri-Motors were still flying, most in Central America. Today, 70 years later, five planes are still flying, five are fully restored in museums and at least two are actively under restoration.

Much has been written about how many

Model T automobile parts were used in the Ford planes. The Model T steering wheel is the part most commonly cited as being used, but Bob Baron, who was an airplane inspector for the entire time Ford planes were being built, states that there were only five common parts. The major item was the Johnson Bar brake lever from the Lincoln. In addition, there were three twist cap reflector lights

Junkers had started using corrugated alluminum, as seen on this Junkers F-13L before World War I. When Ford sent his demonstration planes to Europe in 1929, Junkers sued for patent infringement and won. (HFM 189.3038)

on the instrument panel, four ball caps used on the stabilizer brace strut, the door handle and lock assembly and individual ashtrays which were available on the open market.

Finally, anyone who has seen the Junkers and Fokker airplanes in the Ford Museum can't help but notice Ford's similarity to Junkers' corrugated metal skin and Fokker's engine placement under the wings. The Ford is a high wing, corrugated metal, three-engine monoplane while the Junkers is a low wing, corrugated metal, single engine monoplane.

Junkers had flown his first all metal plane, the J1, in 1915 and Germany had used duralumin, which was a closely guarded secret, in its wartime Zeppelins.

The Fokker, a high wing, three-engine monoplane, had a plywood wing and a tubular steel fuselage covered in fabric. Fokker's single engine passenger planes were well known in Europe, but most Americans connected the Fokker name with the German fighter planes of World War I. In July 1925, Tony Fokker was in the United States to promote the sale of his passenger planes when the first National Air Tour was announced for September 1925. Recognizing the potential publicity of entering the only three-motor aircraft in the Tour, Fokker sent three of the new Wright Whirlwind engines to his Netherlands factory and directed a rush job to bury two of the engines in the leading edge of the wings of his proven FVIIa model, similar to the way Stout was designing his 3AT. Fokker's engineers did not have time for the necessary design and engineering work to meet the September deadline, so they hung the engines under the wings. The resulting performance and publicity was all Fokker hoped for and Ford engineers certainly remembered the Fokker when Stout's 3AT proved to be such a disaster. Harold Hicks, who was head of the air-

Tony Fokker had three of the new Wright J4 engines installed on his successful single engine model F VIIa to compete in the 1925 National Air Tours. Pilots on the tour complained about the blantant advertising on the Fokker plane. (Hudek)

plane design team, in his <u>Oral Reminiscences</u> for Ford's 50th Anniversary commented: *"We did take a profile off the* (Fokker) *wing, but that was never used in the subsequent Ford Tri-Motor plane. We had a standard N.C.A. wing on our plane."*

An interesting comparison of the early Ford and Fokker tri-motor planes was contained in a September 17, 1926 letter from Ernest Greenwood, Department of Commerce, to Major Schroeder: *"My feeling with regard to the fabric fuselage was that if I moved very much I would either put my foot or elbow through it. I am thoroughly sold on metal construction."*

Did Stout and Ford engineers copy these planes? The simple answer is that they recognized Junkers' use of all metal as the wave of the future and used Fokker's idea of hanging the engines under the wings to help slow the landing speed of the new Ford Tri-Motor. They selected good ideas from both.

Chapter 4 - Notes

(1) Bill Stout was undoubtedly the father of the all-metal Air Sedan and Air Pullman, but the design credit (how much is unknown) belongs to George Prudden. In a 1952 letter to Ford Tri-Motor historian Bill Larkins (see preface), Bill Stout wrote regarding the Air Pullman: *"Much credit should be given to George Prudden for having established many of the fundamentals of internal design now used on all planes."(page 51)*

(2) Who designed the Ford Tri-Motor? There is no definitive answer. It looks a great deal like the Stout designed 3AT and some elements were copied, but Stout never claimed credit for it. Several others have and the most thorough discussion is contained in the

Fall 1970 issue of the <u>American Aviation Historical Society Journal.</u> It contains articles from Tom Towle and John Lee, both of whom participated in the design of the airplane. The nearest answer is that a lot of people contributed. *(page 51)*

(3)   In May 1926, the Bureau of Aeronautics was established under the Department of Commerce to determine which pilots and airplanes could fly, however, air services that flew the mail were regulated by the Contract Air Mail routes controlled by the Post Office Department and were told where and when to fly. In July 1934, the name was changed to the Bureau of Air Commerce under the Department of Commerce. In 1938, civil aviation responsibility, fragmented between the Department of Commerce, the Post Office Department and the Interstate Commerce Commission, were combined in the Commerce Department's Civil Aeronautics Authority (CAA). Finally in 1958, with the advent of jet transportation, control of civil aviation was finally given to an independent department with the establishment of the Federal Aviation Agency (FAA). *(page 55)*

(4)   The <u>Future of Flying</u> by Louis Bleriot carried in the <u>Lincoln</u> magazine (a Ford Motor Company publication) August 1926. Bleriot also commented: *"Engineers must know that it is the feeling of possible engine failure which arrests interest in people who, otherwise, are favorably inclined to flying."* *(page 57)*

(5)   Tom Towle, one of the Ford engineers, stated: *"Jimmy Smith told me to go over to the factory Saturday afternoon when no one was there and get all the drawings."* The factory burned down the next day. *"There was little talk about the fire because there was little doubt who had the factory burned, or why!"* John Lee, another Ford engineer commented: *"My guess is that the object was to destroy the Air Pullman (3AT) and whoever was assigned to it was a bit too thorough."* Both comments are in the Fall 1970 issue of the <u>American Aviation Historical Society Journal.</u> *(page 58)*

(6)   In connection with the 50th anniversary of the Ford Motor Company in 1953, over 250 interviews were conducted with current and former long service employees of the company in order to preserve their experiences. These <u>Oral Reminiscences</u> are available in the Henry Ford Museum archives. *(page 58)*

5

NEW FACTORY AND OTHER BUILDINGS

Airplane Factory

By November 1926, the small airplane factory that had so delighted Bill Stout two years earlier, had been replaced with an enormous new factory to produce the new Tri-Motor airplane designed by Ford's engineers. Henry Ford was still the only industrialist with the vision, capital and willingness to invest in an airplane manufacturing facility on such a grand scale. This facility, designed by architect Albert Kahn, was 500 feet long, 124 feet wide and made of Bedford limestone and fire-clay brick. The new factory was 62,000 square feet, three times the size of the destroyed plant, with a steel and glass roof extending the full 124 feet width from wall to wall without intervening supports. This new building, standing partially on the site of the former Stout factory, did not bear the Stout name.

Henry Ford was now committed to building airplanes and his initial plans called for the production of one plane every two weeks produced by the: *"Ford system of progressive production, now to be applied to airplane manufacturing for the first time."* He would build planes like he built cars — on an assembly line. Within two years, plans were being made for producing one plane every two days and in June 1929, it was announced the airplane factory would be more than doubled to 640 feet long

Aerial view of the new Ford airplane factory. Remnants of the Stout factory can be seen on extreme left. New hangar building is on the right. (Hudek 189.6602)

Notice the new addition to the Ford airplane factory building on the left. This addition doubled the size of the building but the Depression of 1929 severely curtailed operations. Concrete runways are prominent in this 1930 photograph. (Hudek 189.7653)

and eighteen were test flown." Ironically, this proved to be the high water mark for Ford airplane production as, from then on, no more than five planes a month would be built.

The <u>Monthly Report of Employees</u> reflects 150 employees working at the airplane plant in November 1926 when they were still

by 258 feet wide (165,120 square feet). This allowed for the consolidation of parts making operations from other locations as well as providing for the maximum production of one plane a day. Four months later, the <u>Ford News</u> (August 1, 1929) announced: *"Production of Ford Tri-Motor all-metal monoplanes broke all existing records during the month of June. A total of twenty-five were trimmed*

working on the first three planes. By December 1928, that number had swelled to just over 1,000 peaking out at 1,455 in July, 1929.[1] With the onset of the depression, the employment number hovered between 200 and 500, finally dropping to an airport maintenance staff of about 35 which was maintained until April 1937, the last monthly report that listed Airplane Plant employees.

The Ford Tri-Motor assembly line. Airplane in the foreground is the first of the larger 5AT models that became the choice aircraft for most airlines of the period. (Hudek)

AVIATION
January 30, 1928

Ford airplanes now built by continuous production methods

THE assembly line, interchangeable parts and uniform products now characterize the production of Ford all-metal, tri-motored, transport monoplanes.

Just as it was the first to apply that method to the manufacture of automobiles, the Ford Motor Company again is one of the first to apply the same ideas to airplane production. This pioneering is proving entirely successful.

From the receiving department at one end of the plant, where sheet duralumin and all rough stock enter, work progresses in a continuous process until the finished plane emerges at the other end, ready for test.

In addition to increasing production to keep pace with orders for Ford planes, this system offers a very definite benefit to future as well as present owners. For it assures the correct fit and easy installation of any replacement parts which may be required, thereby cutting down "out of service" time, and lowering mechanical up-keep costs.

The Stout Metal Airplane Co.
DIVISION OF FORD MOTOR COMPANY
Dearborn, Michigan

In oval: *Motor mounting assembly line*
Below: *Frame of fuselage ready for covering*

Fitting wing covering to a wooden form. All parts must conform exactly to the curvature of the form.

Assembling frame member in a jig. Pilot seats and completed frames at left.

Center wing assembly being lowered into place. Wings were nearly three feet thick and made in three sections allowing damaged tips to be easily repaired. (Hudek 189.6275)

was built on a cantilever plan, extending on each side from a row of steel towers in the center of the building which caused the least obstruction. The old hangar was relegated to maintenance and repair for airplanes operating in the Ford Air Transportation Service and it would later house a wind tunnel with a 42 inch throat for testing scale models. In 1929, the Government located a weather bureau office in the old hangar, sending weather balloons up twice a day from the roof.

The new hangar was the most modern and one of the largest in the world. It held upwards of 20 aircraft. Doors on both sides of the building retracted into the end walls. (HFM 189.4464)

Airplane Hangar

The new airplane factory required a huge new hangar to handle the anticipated requirements generated by the new airplane factory and Bill Stout's new air service. The new hangar, larger and entirely different from any currently existing in the world and capable of housing nearly 20 planes, was underway by March 1926. It was 123 feet long and 300 feet wide, built of buff brick, with 32 steel and glass doors extending the full 300 feet on both sides. All doors were able to fully retract into the ends of the building. The roof

Airport Terminal

To accommodate the new Stout Air Services passenger line, and to handle the needs of

Cantilevered supports running down the center of the hangar provided support for the roof while allowing for maximum flexibility (HFM 189.4534)

Ford's own Air Transportation Service traffic, an airport terminal building was built and opened in November 1927. Looking much like a small train station of the period, it was a two story affair. Constructed of white brick, stone and Spanish tile, it was similar to the new airplane factory. The first floor was 52 feet by 52 feet while the second floor was 28 feet by 28 feet. Offices for both the Ford Air Transport Service and the Stout Air Services operations were on the second floor while a well equipped passenger lounge and ticket office occupied the first floor. A 1928 Ford airport brochure comments: *"we have built a passenger depot which is unique in the country, and which, we believe, is not excelled by any in the world."* Also at this time, the first airport limousine service was started by the Detroit Department of Street Railways to service downtown Detroit and the first hotel airline ticket office in the U.S. was set up in the Book Cadillac hotel in Detroit.

Dearborn Inn

To service air travelers and the soon to be opened Edison Institute — more commonly known as Henry Ford Museum & Greenfield Village — the 108 room Dearborn Inn, designed in the Early American Period style, was opened across the street from the terminal building in July, 1931. Robert Walker, Mayo's secretary, wrote that Edsel Ford, feeling that airlines and everything pertaining to aeronautics was modern, the terminal and inn should also be modern. Edsel won his argument with the terminal but Henry Ford insisted on Early American for the Inn.

Ford Airport terminal building provided offices for the Ford Air Transportation Service and the Stout Air Services on the upper floor. (Edward Hebb) The terminal contained a fully furnished customer lounge and was similar to railroad depots of the day. (Hudek 189.5159)

Dearborn Inn was opened in July 1931 to service airport passengers and visiting Ford employees and dealers. One of the first inns built to handle airline passengers. (Hudek 833.56398.1)

The walls of the main lobby were painted in a panorama of early American history and each piece of furniture was an exact copy of early New England design. The ladies lounge, also distinctively New England, became popular with Detroit society women as a setting for afternoon bridge. Each room, quite small by today's standards, was furnished with antique furniture, a radio and had a modern bathroom. There was the formal Alexandria ballroom, the Early American restaurant and the less formal Ten Eyck Tavern. But there was no cocktail lounge until 1949. A promenade was provided on the roof which afforded the guests an advantageous view: *"where one may watch soaring airplanes and gorgeous sunsets."* The ultra modern kitchen was finished in a new non-tarnishable metal and contained such mar-

vels as dishwashers and electric potato mashers. A contemporary brochure lists: *"Single room with tub and shower — $3.50,"* and *"Through the Dearborn Inn, sightseeing trips in a Ford tri-motored transport plane may be arranged any day except Sunday."* *"A worthy complement to the Ford Airport,"* was how <u>Aero Digest</u> (October 1931) described the Inn, and went on to say it was: *"probably the first modern hotel to be located adjacent to an airport."* [2]

The Oakwood Hotel Company was established as a Ford subsidiary to build the Inn and the Statler Hotel organization was asked to manage it. However, Henry Ford forbade alcoholic beverages and banned smoking, both of which Statler management permitted. Rather than create a confrontation with

Lobby of the Dearborn Inn shows the elegance of the decor which was carried throughout the entire building. (HFM 833.56328.11)

ating loss of $138,436. Land improvements, depreciation and management operating fees would swell the loss to $382,408.

Ford Motor Company continued operating the Dearborn Inn until 1953, when it was donated to the Edison Institute. In 1984, the Edison Institute decided ownership of the Inn was no longer germane to their objectives and the Ford Motor Company repurchased and completely refurbished the Inn, contracting for its operation with the Marriott Corporation.

Henry Ford, they declined the management contract. Management of the Inn was then turned over to the Treadway Corporation, which ran a chain of Early American Inns in the east, including Ford's Wayside Inn in Sudbury, Massachusetts.

As the Fords were aware that air travelers would not provide necessary volume for profitable operations for some time, they planned to use the Inn for visiting Ford employees and Ford dealers. Unfortunately, the Inn had several strikes against it on opening day. By closing the airport on Sundays, Henry Ford had forced commercial aviation to use the newly opened Detroit City Airport and he would shortly abandon his aviation interests. These problems were compounded by the depression that was causing mounting financial chaos across the country and in the first three and one half years of operation, the Dearborn Inn would show an oper-

Radio Beacon and Telephone

In spite of the contention by Smithsonian writers that concrete runways were Ford's most important aviation contribution, the radio beacon was equally as important if not more so. The Radio Beacon proved to be the most far reaching of all Ford patents as it allowed planes to overcome the dangers and cancellations caused by rain, fog and darkness. It permitted planes to find their way from point to point in all types of weather without concern for visual observations and the principle is still in use today.

Ford engineers, proceeding on earlier developmental work by the Bureau of Standards and the U.S. Air Service, but attacking from a different angle, perfected the radio beacon for use in commercial aviation application. The Ford radio beacon transmitted signals alternatively on two sending loops set at a predetermined acute angle. Radio signals were broadcast continuously from the two loops: the letter "A" (dot-dash) from one loop, and letter "N" (dash-dot) from the other. Signals were sent alternately from the two loops in such rapid succession that they interlocked in the center of the angle to form a steady "on course" hum.

The first successful radio guided flight between airfields took place in a snow storm on February 10, 1926. A Ford Tri-Motor flown by Ford pilot Harry Brooks, made a round trip flight between Ford Airport, Dearborn, Michigan and McCook Field, Dayton, Ohio being guided the entire way by radio beacon. The Ford radio beacon was placed in service in October, 1927 and carried the call letters WFO. From that point in time, all Ford Air Transportation Service planes carried radios.

This patented Ford system would prove the bedrock of commercial aviation, allowing for on-time scheduling from virtually any destination to any other destination under most weather conditions. Most importantly, it was given to the aviation industry free of all fees and royalties.

Due to the increase in the use of radios on aircraft and the increased volume of air traffic, a radio telephone ground transmitting station, a project Ford had been experimenting with since 1927, was inaugurated June, 1930 with call letters WQDW. Weather for all Detroit, Cleveland and Chicago flights was broadcast every half hour from 8:25 AM to 4:25 PM, and every fifteen minutes when the weather was bad.

Notes - Chapter 5

(1) John Neville, in his comprehensive eight part article on Ford aviation, published in <u>Aviation</u> magazine in 1929, reported 1,850 employees in early 1929 at the height of Ford's consolidation of operations and expansion of production. This probably included employees producing airplane parts in the Rouge complex. *(page 71)*

(2) Contrary to common belief fostered by reports such as this one and public relations releases by the Inn itself over the years, the Dearborn Inn was not the first hotel built to accommodate air travelers. That honor goes to one opened at the Oakland Airport in California in 1929. *(page 76)*

6

ADVERTISING AND PROMOTION

Advertising

Some aviation writers today have either lost sight of or have never known the value of Henry Ford's reputation and his airplanes in helping to establish the foundation of commercial aviation. They either completely ignore it or treat it in an off hand manner. The impact of Henry Ford and the Ford Tri-Motor on the public's understanding and attitude about safety, dependability and reliability of commercial aviation cannot be ignored. Daring and reckless barnstormers had caused two thirds of all aviation fatalities and, as a result, aviation had an understandably low image in the public mind. Most people thought flying was fine as long as they could keep one foot on the ground. Henry Ford and his airplanes played a major role in convincing a great portion of the public that aviation was more than what barnstormers did on weekends.

It would not be until 1926 that Air Commerce regulations would be issued covering airworthiness standards and licensing requirements for airplanes, pilots and mechanics and they wouldn't take effect until 1928. Henry Ford had made it possible for the average man to own a car and to enjoy the freedom that ownership represented. He was literally worshipped by millions of people around the world. The prevailing attitude was that if Henry Ford, a knowledgeable and successful business man, was involved in this aviation game, it must be OK. Even Will Rogers, the most popular humorist of the day, commented: *"Ford wouldent (sic) leave the ground and take to the air unless things looked good to him up there."*

Ford's first ad promoting aviation and the new all-metal Tri-Motor, was a centerfold in Aviation Magazine (August 15, 1927), declaring: *"The interest and resources of the Ford Motor Company are squarely behind the development of aviation and production of the Ford monoplane."* Between 1927 and 1932, the N. W. Ayers & Son advertising firm of Philadelphia handled Ford's aviation campaign and ran over 100 different ads in major newspapers, aviation magazines and general interest magazines such as: Saturday Evening Post, National Geographic, Literary

Digest, Vanity Fair, American Boy and Time, promoting aviation and Ford airplanes to the general public. The combined circulation of the magazines was over six million, reaching an estimated fifteen to twenty million people in the United States. Newspaper ads added countless millions more. Ford's ad campaign was directed, not only to the ultimate airplane buyer, but to the public at large and stressed the safety, comfort and reliability of aviation, declaring in Aviation magazine (December 1927): *"The public needs to be educated about flying. It cannot, of itself, become air-minded. It wants to be 'sold' aviation. The aviation advertising published in the great national magazines by Ford Motor Company is dedicated to this educational work."*

Ford hammered home in ad after ad the safety, dependability and reliability of modern aircraft piloted by responsible pilots. He continually related the safety and performance records of his own air operations to emphasize his point. In July 1929, Ford sent a large, hard cover book, entitled Lift Up Your Eyes, to 1,000 top executives in the United States. It contained seventeen of Ford's aviation ads with a cover letter stating: *"It was necessary to induce in the minds of the general public an enthusiastic acceptance of the airplane as a common carrier. We were convinced, therefore, that one of the primary needs of commercial aviation was an advertising campaign to reach the general public."*

Aero Digest (March 1928) stated: *"His advertising has done more to popularize flying among the reading public than all the stunts that have ever been stunted, at the risk of neck and limb."* And in 1928 Ford was awarded the prestigious Harvard Advertising Award: *"for the excellence of their planning and execution in advertising both the Ford Motor Car and the general subject of aviation."* Years later, Ford aviation advertising was included in the book The 100 Greatest Advertisements published by Julian Watkins in 1949.

A parallel target of Ford's advertising to the average man was the potential of commercial aviation to operators and businessmen. While preaching the safety of all-metal, three engine planes to the public, he was emphasizing to business the reliability, dependability, economy and ease of maintenance of the all-metal Ford plane as proved in thousands of miles of service in the Ford Air Transportation Service and he always offered to share his experiences with others.

While aviation magazines of the period were full of airplane, airplane engine and airplane equipment manufacturer ads touting the value of their particular merchandise, none of them pushed the safety of aviation as widely and aggressively as did Henry Ford.

The last Ford aviation ad appeared in October 1932, appropriately enough, offering used planes for sale.

Safety wins the Traffic

TRAFFIC volume, as the air mail has proved, always follows a record for safety and reliability. Competing air-lines between London and Paris show that passengers select the route with the greatest safety record. The rule of safety applies equally to all air loads. Safety wins the traffic!

The plane which places least dependence on the human element approaches closest to absolute safety. That is the principle on which the Ford Tri-motored Transport is designed and built. It reduces dependence on human performance to the minimum.

There is vast reserve power for quick take-offs and climb. This makes maximum allowance for errors in judgment and for overcoming extreme conditions or emergencies. The power is divided into three separate units, any two of which will maintain flight in the rare case of failure of the third. With Wright Whirlwind engines a known and thoroughly demonstrated reliability of power is assured.

The Ford Tri-motored Transport can be controlled on the ground with the certainty of an automobile. Independently acting brakes permit steering without "ground-looping" in cross winds; they bring the plane to a quick stop where small fields demand it, without tendency to nose over; in all work on the ground they dispense with the need of handling crew.

The all-metal construction gives a known-strength material and eliminates the danger of hidden deterioration of materials such as glue and fabric. Careful and frequent inspection is encouraged by the accessibility of all parts of the structure, including the interior of the wings.

Gasoline is kept in tanks suspended in the wings, away from engines, crew and passengers — this, with all-metal construction, removes the fire hazard even under the most extreme conditions.

The inherent stability of the plane permits flight with "hands off" in smooth air and removes any danger of spinning from a stall or a side slip if these should be done either accidentally or intentionally. Here is an advance not only over military ships, but also over all commercial performance.

Even the entrance door has been so placed that there is no excuse for either passengers or crew going near the propellers!

Safety and reliability! These are first considerations in the Ford monoplane —in research, in design, in experimental work, and in the final building. Safety in every condition the plane can meet. No plane has ever placed so little dependence on human watchfulness, care and skill.

THE STOUT METAL AIRPLANE CO.
Division of Ford Motor Company
Dearborn, Michigan

Why Ford monoplanes
are made entirely
of metal

THE purpose of commercial planes is earnings. Naturally, these come only after all expenses. Consequently the first step is keeping expense at the minimum. Reduction of expense to the air-line operator is one of the reasons Ford monoplanes are built entirely of metal.

The metal that goes into Ford monoplanes does not deteriorate as wood and fabric must. It doesn't rot or warp, stretch or tear. Right there is a reduction in maintenance. Also assurance of more continuous service.

Fit of replacements is another advantage. Every part of a Ford monoplane can be replaced direct from stock with no time or labor expense in adjusting to fit. An hour of ground-work saved is an hour your plane can be in the air—earning . . . maintaining schedules.

Here is another saving you may not have considered. Wood varies widely in strength. One piece of wood will stand forty thousand pounds. Another, apparently exactly like it, breaks at twenty-five thousand. A wide safety-margin must be allowed. That is weight which takes the place of pay-load. Metal, on the other hand, can be accurately gauged, and excessive safety-margins are not needed. The greatest possible percentage of your lift is carrying profit-paying loads.

The superior rigidity and strength of metal wing construction removes the need for many trusses and braces inside, and struts and wires outside. Not only is the final weight lighter than wood and fabric construction, but also parasite resistance is greatly reduced; lift and speed are both increased.

The use of all-metal construction is but one of the many instances of the steps taken to make Ford monoplanes capable for successful and continuous air-line operation. A more complete idea of how Ford monoplanes meet the needs of air-line operators may be obtained from our new booklet, "The New Era of Transportation," which will be mailed to you upon request. In addition, this booklet contains much valuable information gained from practical experience in operating the Ford air-lines. If still more information is desired on any phase of experimental or operations work connected with commercial flying or airplane building, it will be furnished to any who wish it, free of cost or obligation.

THE STOUT METAL AIRPLANE CO.
Division of Ford Motor Company
Dearborn, Michigan

National Air Tours

The idea for the first air tour in 1925 was inspired by the tremendous public reaction and results of the Glidden Auto Tours which were started in 1904 to promote highway travel and development in the United States. The Detroit Board of Commerce and The Detroit Aviation Society, of which Mayo was President and Edsel Ford a Director, decided an air tour emphasizing and demonstrating the reliability and safety of commercial air transportation would be just the vehicle for attracting the public's attention to the serious side of aviation and stimulate the construction of local airfields. Their decision was nearly simultaneous with the passage of the Kelly Air Mail Act in February 1925 authorizing the Post Office Department to contract with private carriers for the transportation of airmail. The Fords helped organize the tour by donating $50,000 and offering the use of Ford Airport. In addition, Edsel Ford donated the magnificent trophy shown on the cover of this book. Made of sterling silver, it is 36 inches high and mounted on a marble base. The trophy would be permanently awarded to the first manufacturer to win the tour five times (later changed to three). This trophy, called *The Edsel B. Ford Trophy,* took nine months for the silversmiths to create and was truly a trophy worth striving for. Initially the tour was promoted as the Commercial Airplane Reliability Tour, but was, due to the Fords' involvement, commonly referred to as the Ford Reliability Tour or Ford Air Tour.

The Edsel B. Ford Trophy, 36 inches high and made of sterling silver, was designed for the National Air Tours. It is currently on display in the Henry Ford Museum. (HFM B.114743)

By 1927, the tour would be known officially as the National Air Tour.

The official rules, while quite involved, were based primarily on the weight carried in proportion to the weight of the plane and the plane's ability to take off and land in the fewest seconds and maintain the most consistent speed over the measured distance, again in proportion to the weight of the plane.

Start of the first National Air Tour in 1925. Corner of the Stout Metal Airplane Company factory is seen in the upper left corner. Conditions at Ford Airport caused some to call it *Lake Ford*. (Hudek 833.44186)

Once the participating cities were selected, but before the tour could begin, however, someone had to find out where the planes would land. As previously mentioned, most communities had no airfields and those that did could be anything from a farmer's pasture to the county fairgrounds, but never an airfield as we know it today. A pathfinder trip was undertaken to find and mark these fields and provide local officials with three pages of detailed instructions covering such items as a map of the landing field, field markings, wind socks, aviation gas, mechanics, food, police, judges, referees and last but not least, publicity.

First Tour — 1925

The first tour featured seventeen planes from eleven manufacturers with all, but the Fokker

tri-motor, being single engine planes powered by pre-war or war-time engines. Tony Fokker, to the annoyance of manny of the participants, tried, with some success, to turn the 1925 tour into what some contestants referred to as the *Fokker Publicity Tour*. Fokker's antics started, according to The New York World (September 22, 1925), when flying low over Henry Ford's home, Fokker dropped his calling card on the front lawn. His plane was painted up like a flying billboard with the Fokker name visible from any angle while all other participants had a small company name sign painted on the tail, side or engine cowling. With the new Ford Tri-Motor poised to entered the competition in 1926, Fokker never entered a plane in another tour.

Starting September 28, 1925, tour planes flew

This silver medallion was awarded to all National Air Tour participants who finished the 1925 tour with a perfect score. The rim of the medallion reads: EDSEL B. FORD RELIABILITY TOUR FOR THE DEVELOPMENT OF COMMERCIAL AVIATION. Pilot's name and type of plane was engraved on the reverse side. (Hudek 833.46373)

a prescribed six day route of 1,775 miles, visiting 13 cities in the Midwest. The <u>Detroiter</u> magazine (September 28, 1925) kicked the tour off on the day of the race with a banner headline in a feature article: *"The Greatest Week In Commercial Aviation."* There were thousands of people at Ford Airport to give the flyers a tremendous send off and the reception was the same at every city visited. Major aerial events were staged at Ford Airport during the tour, including demonstrations by airplanes of the Army's 1st Pursuit Squadron from Selfridge Field, Michigan and bombers from McCook Field, Ohio. It was certainly a spectacular scene with the largest assembly of commercial airplanes anyone had ever seen. Daily events scheduled at the airport included free balloon rides, free trips to the top of the Ford mooring mast, dead-stick landing contests and watching the Ford airplanes leave and arrive on their daily trips to and from Chicago and Cleveland. As each event was to be described in detail to the spectators, there were 252 amplifying horns deployed around the field, representing the largest such installation ever made. October 4th, the final day of the tour, was even grander with 35,000 people on hand to welcome the heroes back. Events scheduled for that day started with balloon chasing in the morning, followed by 'Apron String' contests, 'Pony Express' races and, in the afternoon more ballooning activities. The arrival of the tour planes scheduled for 4:00 to 5:00 PM were to be followed by the start of the Trophy Balloon Race. The balloon race, sponsored by the <u>Detroit News,</u> was dedicated to the encouragement of the study of air currents: *"which in a sudden rage demolished the gigantic Shenandoah in midair."* Although the arrival ceremonies were marred and delayed by rain storms, the crowd remained and went wild when the planes finally showed up. Ford cameramen filmed the crowds in a downpour carrying the arriving pilots away on their shoulders. The competition ended with a grand dinner in the Ford hangar.

Contrary to many assertions that the Fokker airplane won the race, there was no winner. Each of the eleven participants, finishing with a perfect score, received a cash prize of $350, had their name engraved on the Ford trophy and were presented with a large silver medallion engraved with their name and the name of their plane. The Ford Air Transportation Service 2AT plane, piloted by Edward Hamilton, made the best time for this first tour, with an average speed of 101.5 mph. No other plane reached 100 mph.

The consensus among the towns visited during the tour was that this was the grandest aerial exhibition they had ever seen (in most cases it was the first) and set the stage for future tours. Most importantly it created the awareness in local authorities for the need for airfields. By the following year, many towns and cities had built, were building or were planning to build real airfields and were vying to have their towns added to future Air Tour stops.

One result of the first tour was a program to get towns to identify themselves from the air. Edsel Ford wrote to all Ford dealers in December 1925, stating: *"It seems that one of the very great difficulties of cross-country flying is in trying to distinguish over what town or city the pilot is traveling. Therefore, will you not paint on the roof of your garage the name of the city or town in which you are located? Also, an arrow, pointed due north should be painted immediately following the name of the city or town."*

Unfortunately, Edsel Ford recommended the size of the letters be four feet high. Eight months later, the Army Air Service determined that, while signs this size were clearly visible at 1,000 feet, they were completely invisible at 3,000 feet, the minimum altitude required of heavier-than-air craft flying over thickly populated areas, and recommended letters twelve feet high.[1]

Second Tour — 1926

The second tour, again through the midwest, which started August 7, 1926, was even larger and longer with 16 manufacturers entering 25 planes. Crowds gathered at the airport by 6:30 AM to inspect the airplanes and 15,000 people were on hand to wave the planes off at 9:00 AM. As no other multiple engine plane was entered this year, Ford chose to refrain from officially entering his new Tri-Motor plane. Due to the public interest, as evidenced by the various cities trying to participate, the duration of the tour was extended to two weeks to give the plane manufacturers more time to show and demonstrate their planes at the various stops. This tour covered 2,585 miles in 14 days with stops at 14 cities. New rules were established this year, which would prevail for the balance of the tours. A $2,500 first prize would be based on total points earned for various activities. Lesser amounts were awarded to all others

The Gordon Bennett balloon races, such as this one at the 1928 National Air Tour, generated a great deal of publicity. They attracted many observers and filled in the days between the start of the race and the return of the planes. The young boy sitting by the camera is Henry Ford II, son of Edsel Ford. (HFM 189.5742)

who finished the tour. Walter Beech in a Travel Air 4000 bi-plane, with an average speed of 124.1 mph, won the top prize of $2,500.

Third Tour — 1927

1927 was a difficult year for Henry Ford. He had lost car sales leadership to Chevrolet and on May 25th, the last of 15 million Model Ts rolled off the line. Ford announced that after 19 years his cherished Model T would be discontinued in favor of the new Model A, which would not appear until early 1928. All of the Ford factories would close for the next seven months. In spite of his car problems Ford pushed ahead with his aviation interests. The third National Air Tour, which

started June 27th, proved to be the largest of them all, coming as it did just weeks after Charles Lindbergh's trip to Paris. In 1926 and 1927, interest in aviation had been stirred up by other famous aviators who had also captured the public's attention with their aerial explorations—pilots such as Charles Nungessor, George Wilkins, Clarence Chamberlain and Richard Byrd, as well as the rescue of the *Bremen* flyer by Bernt Balchen and Floyd Bennett. Also, in the months leading up to the tour, the country had been kept in suspense with the constant publicity surrounding the plans of the numerous aviators who hoped to capture the $25,000 prize[2] offered for the first non-stop flight from New York to Paris. Aviation awareness literally exploded when Charles Lindbergh claimed the prize on May 21, 1927. The Lindbergh celebrations continued for months and added greatly to the public's interest in the National Air Tour. This year would see great improvement in the airplanes entered. Over two thirds of the planes would be using the new Wright Whirlwind air-cooled radial engine and most would be equipped with brakes for the first time. Cabin planes and monoplanes were be-

Fourth Tour — 1928

By the start of the fourth tour on June 30, 1928, there were over 360 municipal airports and over 300 private and commercial airports and many cities were clamoring to be included on the tour. Twenty-five planes were entered this year for the stated purpose, which differed little from the prior tours: *"to dem-*

Finish of the 1930 National Air Tour at Ford Airport. The number 6 Ford was the winner of this year's race. The new Ford Museum in the background was not opened to the public until 1933. (HFM 833.55468.2)

coming more popular although nearly two thirds would still be open cockpit planes. An enthusiastic crowd of over 30,000 watched the fourteen flyers depart Ford Airport for cities as far away as Omaha, Oklahoma City and Dallas, and similar crowds welcomed them at every stop. That year, Edward Stinson in his Stinson SM-1 monoplane, with an average speed of 124.3 mph, won the top prize of $2,500.

onstrate the reliability and practicality of commercial aviation under everyday travel conditions and to promote public acceptance of flying in general." This was the longest tour, proceeding from Dearborn, Michigan to San Antonio, Texas, to San Diego, California, to Tacoma, Washington and back to Dearborn, Michigan covering 6,304 miles in 29 days. An estimated 175,000 people visited Ford Airport during the festivities which

Last day of the last race in July 1931. Although public interest had declined over the years, it is not obvious looking at all the cars on Oakwood Boulevard and parked in the lower left of this picture. Balloon races were still being held, sponsored this year by the <u>Detroit News.</u> (Detroit News photo)

included the 17th Gordon Bennett International Balloon Race, the first national contest of the Airplane Model League of America and other crowd pleasing events. Estimates indicate that more than a million persons had witnessed the tour in various cities. Missoula, Montana with a population of 16,000 had, by actual count, 12,066 persons turn out to greet the flyers. The winner this year was John Wood in a Waco Ten averaging 128.1 mph.

Fifth Tour — 1929

Interest was waning in 1929 and while it was the biggest tour ever, the arrival of the planes didn't turn out the crowds as in past years. Twenty-nine planes participated in the tour starting October 5th and covered 5,017 miles, as they visited 31 cities in the midwest and east coast. This tour was won by John Livingston in his Waco CSO averaging 130.8 mph.

Sixth Tour — 1930

The 1930 Tour with 18 participants, left Ford Airport on September 11, and covered 4,814 miles in the midwest and central Canada visiting 29 cities. The lack of public enthusiasm was very noticeable with few records in the Ford archives and few reports in newspapers

This Ford display at the Detroit Air Show in 1931 featured a paper mache giant holding the model 13AT. The single engine model 8AT is to the right. (Hudek 189.8621)

of the time. Ford Pilot Harry Russell in a Ford Tri-Motor won with an average speed of 131.9 mph.

Seventh Tour — 1931

The seventh and final tour started July 4, 1931 and attracted only 14 entrants from nine manufacturers. The tour included 32 cities and covered 4,816 miles in 21 days. The tour was less than spectacular as evidenced by the fact that press coverage was limited and even in the Ford archives there are virtually no records or photographs. Again Harry Russell in a Ford Tri-Motor won with an average speed of 143.2 mph.

By now, the Depression was setting in. Ford wasn't selling many planes or cars and his airplane factory, along with other famous airplane makers of the period, such as Travel

This flyer was passed out by Ford dealers to encourage customers to visit a local airport for a 25 mile aerial tour of their city for $5.00. The Ford Tri-Motor represented modern barnstorming in safe metal airplanes with reliable pilots. This tour was instituted by Ford dealers to generate traffic for their dealerships. (O'Callaghan collection)

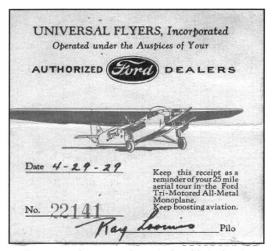

Passenger's souvenir stub for flight in the Ford Tri-Motor airplane sponsored by the local Ford dealer. (O'Callaghan collection)

Souvenir stub issued by Clyde Ice, prominent pilot who barnstormed a Ford Tri-Motor in the central United States. He wrote Ford officials inquiring about the possibilities of looping the big aircraft. (O'Callaghan collection)

Air, Buhl, Bird and Great Lakes, had closed for all practical purposes. Money was scarce everywhere, and by now, many people had seen big planes and the tours just died for lack of interest. Many greats of the aviation world had taken part in these tours and, Ford planes having won in 1925, 1930 and 1931,

Ford Motor Company took possession of The Edsel B. Ford Trophy placing it on permanent display in the Henry Ford Museum. Although the public had lost interest in watching big planes come and go, they were now caught up with speed. Their attention was now riveted to shows like the annual Chicago and Cleveland air races.

All tours had started and finished at Ford Airport and during this period Ford had spent lavishly in advertising the benefits and safety of commercial aviation. Although not mentioning the air tours, this heavy advertising schedule did much to attract favorable public attention to Ford.

Other Promotional Activity

While many people over 50 can remember being parked at the edge of an airfield with their parents watching the planes take off and land, it is still difficult to imagine how intense the public interest was in aviation in the 1920s. The Detroit News estimated thousands turned out for the arrival of the Navy's airship Los Angeles in 1926 and they couldn't count the crowds when Lindbergh arrived at Ford Airport in July 1927.[3] By 1928, newspaper reports, which appear to be exagerated, estimated visitors to Ford Airport ranged from 150 daily in the winter to 2,000 daily in the summer. Tours were available including the factory and hangar where Ford had on display Byrd's North Pole Fokker airplane, the *Josephine Ford*, Brock and

Schlee's world traveler Stinson airplane the *Pride of Detroit* and an early 1909 Bleriot airplane, similar to one that first crossed the English Channel in 1909.

Ford automobile dealers got into the act, too. In 1928, Leo Rocca, a partner in a Washington, DC, Ford and Lincoln dealership organized Universal Flyers Inc. Universal Flyers purchased a new Ford Tri-Motor to promote the dealership by taking customers for rides and the first month carried over 4,000 passengers. This was the first step in a plan to send the plane on a tour of the United States under sponsorship of local Ford and Lincoln dealers. Flyers were passed out stating: *"Your Local Ford Dealer Invites You to FLY. Enjoy a 25 mile aerial tour for $5.00."* Tickets for a ride, only available at the local Ford dealer's showroom, provided many thousands of passengers with their first airplane ride, and many more in the smaller towns with their first view of an airplane.[4] The little paper souvenir flight stubs passed out to the passengers were kept as keen mementos for years. While these flights had the flavor of the old barnstormer, this was a new airplane built by Henry Ford and flown by well trained, reliable pilots. In the Depression years of the early 1930s, interest in aviation was still there, but the price had come down. The Inman Brothers Flying Circus in Humphrey, Nebraska, offered rides in their Ford Tri-Motor for 50¢ in the morning and $1 in the afternoon.

While Ford took advantage of most opportunities to promote aviation in general and Ford Airport and airplanes in particular, Ford's position was that they would not endeavor to sell Ford planes for transoceanic flights and were not particularly interested in stunt flying of any kind. Probably unknown to Mayo or the Fords, Leroy Manning, then Manager of airport operations, replied to Clyde Ice, a well known aviator who had just purchased a new Ford Tri-Motor: *"regarding your proposed plan to loop your Ford plane, I could not officially, of course, approve any such maneuvers. However, I have looped these ships on a number of occasions."* After discussing the problems that could be encountered, Manning closed with: *"If you plan to stunt your ship as a regular thing, why don't you let us put a removable cockpit roof on your ship, and buy yourself a good parachute?"*

In 1932, Harold Johnson purchased a Ford 4AT model and began a career as the premier daredevil Ford Tri-Motor stunt pilot, thrilling thousands of visitors at the annual Cleveland Air Races and other shows throughout the country with spins and dives and snap rolls at tree top level. His ultimate feat performed in 1937 was a reported series of 37 consecutive loops. It was truly a testimony to the inherent strength of the Ford Tri-Motor airplane.

In connection with the National Air Tour of 1925, Ford promoted and hosted the first

Commercial Aeronautical Exposition at Ford Airport, with over 70 vendors displaying their wares. In addition, the <u>Detroit News</u> sponsored an annual balloon race in 1925 and 1926, commencing with the return of the Tour flyers. In 1927, in association with the National Air Tour, Ford Airport was host to the famous Gordon Bennett International Balloon Races, started in 1906 by Gordon Bennett, Jr., the owner of the <u>New York Herald</u> newspaper. So successful was the 1927 balloon race, that it was again held at Ford Airport in 1928, the first time the Gordon Bennett race had ever been held at the same place in successive years.

This is the hand painted identification plate affixed to the first plane Ford sold commercially to the John Wanamaker Co. in New York City. Prior to the sale of this plane, there was no need for a manufacture's nameplate as all planes that had been built were used in Ford's own Air Transportation Service with the Ford name painted under the wings, on the fuselage and on the tail. (Hudek 189.3085)

In September 1930, a Ford Tri-Motor, piloted by Leroy Manning, set a speed record for heavy transport planes with a 4,409 pound load, of 164.4 mph over a 100 kilometer (62.3 miles) closed course between Ford Airport and Ann Arbor, Michigan. In the same month, Manning piloted a Ford 5AT model to first place in the multi-engine transport race at the National Air Races in Chicago with an average speed of 144 mph. And finally, in another first, Harold Lloyd's motion picture, Speedy, was shown in a Ford Tri-Motor flying over Los Angeles in May 1928. A silent film, naturally, considering the decibel count in a flying Ford.

This is the permanent metal manufacturer's nameplate used on all Ford airplanes until November 1928. (Hudek)

In April 1928, the Junkers airplane, *Bremen* made the first successful east-west crossing of the Atlantic, starting in Dublin, Ireland and ending with a landing on Greenly Island, Labrador, damaging the landing gear. Richard Byrd was approached by the New York World newspaper to use the Ford Tri-Motor being prepared for his South Pole flight for a rescue mission. Byrd was well aware of the value of the publicity surrounding a rescue mission by his pilots Floyd Bennett and Bernt Balchen in the Ford Tri-Motor he planned to use. Byrd's plane however, was being refitted with a larger nose engine and could not be readied in time. Ford took another plane being prepared for Sky View Lines of Detroit, Michigan and leased it to the New York World for the trip. Both of Byrd's pilots left sick beds in Detroit to make the flight. Bennett, becoming deathly ill with pneumonia, was hospitalized in Quebec. In a dramatic nighttime flight from New York, Charles Lindbergh made a mercy flight through a raging blizzard, with special serum in a failed attempt to save his life. Balchen went on alone to effect the rescue. Even with the new parts, the *Bremen* could not be flown off the island and was finally brought out by ship. With nothing left to do, Balchen returned with the three *Bremen* flyers in his Ford plane. The City of New York, after a fine reception for the heroes, named its new municipal airport Floyd Bennett Field. The *Bremen* and its crew were later feted by Henry and Edsel Ford at a gala reception at Ford Airport.

Identification

As Henry Ford had acquired all airplanes built by the Stout Metal Airplane Company and placed them in his own Air Transportation Service, they were all marked with large Ford script on both sides of the fuselage and tail and carried large block F O R D letters under the wings. As a result, no identification plate was needed on the planes. However, when the first commercial sale of an Air Transport was made to the John Wanamaker Company in October 1925, some form of permanent Ford identification became desirable. Accordingly, an 18 by 12 inch metal oval medallion with a winged Ford in the center, surrounded by the wording *The Stout Metal Airplane Company*, was designed and placed on the nose of the aircraft. The medallion was placed on all aircraft built through November 1928. The medallion was located near the nose on the early production planes and beside the passenger door on later planes, obviously to create greater passenger awareness. The Stout Metal Airplane Company name continued to be used in advertisements until December 1929. Robert Walker, Mayo's secretary, claimed the elimination of Stout's name in advertising was prompted, not only by Ford's desire to profit from any publicity, but also the feeling that the identification of the Ford name with aviation, via the Ford Tri-Motor, would prove more beneficial to the aviation industry than the continued use of the Stout name.

General Motors' Reaction

As a result of Ford's growing success in his aviation venture, emphasized by the public attention to his Flivver and Byrd's polar flights, General Motors was persuaded that the aviation manufacturing field was too important to ignore. As Alfred Sloan, President of General Motors stated in his biography: *"Aviation was to be one of the greatest growth industries — talk about developing a Flivver plane for everyday family use had unforeseeable consequences for the automobile industry."* Although General Motors' General Aviation Corporation controlled Trans World Airlines (TWA) and later Eastern Airlines, they felt the need to be involved in aircraft manufacturing as well. Accordingly, on March 3, 1931, they purchased effective controlling interest in Western Air Express which gave them control of the Fokker Aircraft Corp, the only direct competitor to the Ford Tri-Motor. Unfortunately, it was just in time for the Great Depression. Also Knute Rockne's death in the crash of a wooden-wing Fokker Tri-Motor on March 31, 1931, signaled the end of the wood and fabric aircraft for passenger service. [5]

Notes - Chapter 6

(1) The town identification project was aggressively supported by the influential Daniel Guggenheim Fund for the Promotion of Aeronautics (1926 -1929), and in February 1934 pursued by the Aeronautics Branch of the Department of Commerce. By the end of 1929, 4,074 communities had completed their identification with another 2,000 indicating they were in the process of doing so. Fifteen years later however, with the outbreak of World War II, the Department of Commerce's Airmarking Specialists were on a crash program to obliterate all topographical identification that was visible from the air. *(page 87)*

(2) Raymond Ortega, a New York hotel owner had first offered the prize in 1919, but it wasn't until 1927 that planes, and engines, capable of the challenge were available. *(page 88)*

(3) Applications for pilot's and aviation mechanic's licenses are a good indication of Lindbergh's impact on the public's awareness of aviation. The 12 months before his flight, 1,800 applications for pilots' licenses had been received by the Department of Commerce. In the 12 months following his flight, 5,500 applications were received.

Applications for aviation mechanics licenses also jumped from 1,600 to 4,700. *(page 92)*

(4) Roscoe Sheller, an old time Ford dealer gives a graphic description in his book <u>Me and the Model T</u>, of the excitement caused in his small town of Sunnyside, Washington, when he arranged for a Ford Tri-Motor to visit and offer rides for $3.00 a person. Most of his neighbors had never seen any airplane, much less a giant one like the Ford. *(page 93)*

(5) Ironically, Ernest Breech, a General Motors executive deeply involved in the management of General Motors' aviation subsidiaries, would become an executive of Ford Motor Company following World War II. As the Chief Operating Executive and later Chairman of the Board, Breech would be instrumental in helping young Henry Ford II save the Ford Motor Company from financial disaster. *(page 96)*

7

POLAR EXPEDITIONS

George Wilkins - Arctic Expedition

Among aerial adventurers in the 1920s, exploring the arctic was almost as popular as trying to cross the Atlantic Ocean. In December 1925, the Detroit Aviation Society, under the Presidency of William Mayo, planned, organized and financed the Detroit Artic Expedition. This was to be a trip to the North Pole for the purpose of exploring and crossing the Pole by air to demonstrate the existence of a short commercial air route over the top of the globe. Captain George Wilkins, a noted Australian explorer, was to command the expedition and Lieutenant Commander Richard Byrd would be invited to be second in command. Edsel Ford had contributed $5,000 to the expedition and it had been planned that the new Ford Tri-Motor (3AT), then under construction, would participate as a backup plane to two Fokker aircraft. The January 1926 fire at the Stout Metal Airplane factory had ended that plan.

In the meantime, while considering Wilkins' offer to be second in command, Byrd had continued in his own preparations for flying to the North Pole. In a January 1926 letter to

Edsel Ford, thanking him for his $20,000 contribution towards his own upcoming Arctic expedition, Byrd advised Ford of his decision to decline the invitation by Wilkins. It proved to be a wise decision as Wilkins' two Fokkers were damaged in forced landings causing the venture to run over budget and postponing his Artic attempt. In December 1926 the Wilkins expedition was soliciting aditional funds so that it could proceed with its Arctic trip, but Edsel Ford declined to make further contributions as he had by now committed his efforts and funds to Bryd's Arctic efforts.[1]

Richard E. Byrd - Arctic Expedition

In March 1925, Admiral William Moffett, Chief of Naval Aviation, who had first met Henry Ford in 1922 at the National Air Races, wrote him to introduce Lieutenant Commander Richard Byrd and his proposed trip to the North Pole, stating: *"I think that Byrd has the ability and determination to succeed in this undertaking, and I want to assure you that you could make no mistake in putting*

Richard Byrd had planned to use the Ford Tri-Motor model 3AT for his North Pole flight but when it was destroyed in the Stout Metal Airplane Company factory fire, he chose the Fokker. Anthony Fokker was concerned that the *Josephine Ford* name on the airplane would be more prominent than his own and insisted on the massive identification shown here. (Hudek 189.5391)

the utmost confidence in him. He is the kind who enjoys life most when there are difficulties to overcome."

The Fords, especially Edsel, were taken with Byrd and the plans for his Arctic venture and became actively engaged in furthering his efforts. Few people are aware of just how responsible Edsel Ford was for the success of Richard Byrd's Arctic and Antarctic

Edsel Ford (right) greeting Commander Richard Byrd (center) and his pilot Floyd Bennett. Byrd and Bennett had just landed at Ford Airport to turn Byrd's Fokker airplane over to Edsel Ford who purchased it for the planned Henry Ford Museum, where it is currently on display. (HFM 0.4448)

Expeditions. For a number of years following World War I, the Army and Navy air services had competed with each other in raising Congressional and public aviation awareness by massive feats of airmanship. By 1926, budgets were running low and, while Naval aviation supported and encouraged Richard Byrd's proposed expeditions due to of Byrd's effort. Byrd had also hoped to use the new Ford 3AT Tri-Motor for his polar trip but the factory fire eliminated that possibility. This left only the Fokker plane, and in gratitude for Ford's assistance, Byrd named the Fokker plane *Josephine Ford* after Edsel Ford's young daughter. Anthony Fokker, well aware of the potential competi-

Ford Tri-Motor 4AT-15 used by Richard Byrd in his flight over the South Pole. Plane was donated for Byrd's expedition by Edsel Ford. It is on display at the Henry Ford Museum, Dearborn, Michigan. (Hudek)

the great publicity value versus Army aviation, the peacetime Navy had no funds to support it. Through his personal financial contributions and encouragement and solicitation of other prominent businessmen, Edsel Ford proved to be the underlying financial force in Byrd's ventures. In January 1926, Edsel Ford not only sent Byrd a check for $20,000, but solicited a like amount from John D. Rockefeller Jr. Ford and Rockefeller were among the most generous supporters tion posed by Ford's aviation efforts with his Tri-Motor plane, was concerned that the Ford name would be more prominent on the airplane than his own and insisted that the Fokker name be displayed so that it would be dominant. Byrd wrote Edsel Ford in April 1926: *"Mr. Fokker has written his name all over the plane, but I could not help that, as he said he would not sell it to me unless I allowed him to do so."*

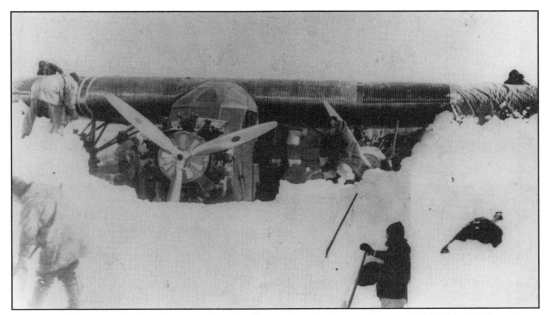

Ford Tri-Motor being dug out after the first winter in Antarctica. (Hudek B.112478 and Hudek B.112479)

A few days later, Byrd wrote Edsel Ford again: *"The whole thing would have been impossible without your backing and encouragement. I owe a great deal to a great many people, but I owe more to you than all the rest put together."*

Following completion of the North Pole trip (May 8, 1926), Ford purchased the Fokker airplane for the planned Henry Ford Museum for $30,000. This would be the first aircraft acquired for Ford's museum.

Richard E. Byrd - Antarctic Expedition

Edsel Ford contributed about $100,000 in cash and materials to Byrd's Antarctic trip and had again written letters to other influential people requesting their financial assistance for Byrd's new effort. Again, John D. Rockefeller, Jr. came through with a $100,000 contribution matching Edsel Ford's, although he asked Edsel to keep his contribution a secret. By then, the Ford Tri-Motor was a reality and Byrd's only choice considering Edsel Ford's backing, although he had ordered a Fokker before he was assured of the availability of the Ford plane. In September 1927, Byrd informed Edsel Ford that he had tried to cancel the Fokker he had ordered but that Tony Fokker had refused: *"Fokker and Llorillard Spencer, President of the Company, admitted to me in New York the other day that should I use a Ford plane it would be a terrible blow to them. I have put Fokker on the map in this country and*

now he won't do me the courtesy to cancel the contracts I have made with him, even though he admitted that he had more orders than he could possibly fill." [2]

The Ford Tri-Motor used in the Antarctic expedition was named the *Floyd Bennett* in memory of Byrd's deceased Arctic expedition pilot. It was built with celluloid windows, thinner gauge skin for the fuselage and parts of the wings to reduce weight and tanks for 691 gallons of gas versus a normal capacity of 235 gallons. The plane was equipped with Ford built skis of ash and hickory sheathed in brass, and the upper wing surface was painted yellow for visibility in case of an emergency landing. In addition, the standard 220 hp Wright Whirlwind center engine was replaced with a 525 hp Wright Cyclone engine with a three bladed prop, as testing in northern Canada proved the need for more power in the high altitudes in which they planned to operate.

Following the successful crossing of the South Pole on November 30, 1929, the plane was left behind, buried in the ice and snow until 1935, when Byrd returned to the Antarctic and retrieved it at the request of Edsel Ford. While the plane was well preserved in the snow, some damage was done to the thin skin of the plane in digging it out and chipping off the ice. It was returned to Floyd Bennett Field, Long Island, New York in August 1935. It was completely dismantled, packed in 25 crates, and trans-shipped on the

Byrd's Antarctica Ford Tri-Motor airplane on display in the Henry Ford Museum, Dearborn, Michigan. (O'Callaghan collection)

Ford canal boat *SS Edgewater* arriving in Dearborn in September 1935. Although not restored, it was reconditioned by the remaining slim crew at the Airplane Division and placed on display in the Henry Ford Museum where it is currently housed along with Byrd's Arctic Fokker airplane the *Josephine Ford*. As a way of acknowledging Edsel Ford's contribution to his efforts, Byrd named one of the newly discovered mountains in the Antarctic after Edsel Ford and another after his daughter Josephine.

While the Fords certainly participated in these ventures from a civic sense, they also undoubtedly sensed the publicity value of a successful expedition. Certainly the publicity surrounding the Arctic Expedition led to their much greater involvement in the Antarctic Expedition.

Notes - Chapter 7

(1) Captain Wilkins was to accomplish his objective of a complete crossing of the Arctic polar basin in 1928 and receive many honors, including Knighthood from King George V of Great Britain. By that time, Richard Byrd had made his own epic flight over the North Pole. *(page 98)*

(2) Byrd finally sold the Fokker to Mrs. Frederick Guest, the American wife of the British Secretary for Air. The plane was named the *Friendship* and was used to fly the first woman across the Atlantic ocean in June 1929. That woman was an unknown aviatrix by the name of Amelia Earhart. *(page 102)*

8

INTERNATIONAL SALES

European Ventures

European subsidization and protection of their aviation industry had become very sophisticated by 1929, and it must have been with a certain amount of apprehension that Henry Ford decided to send one of his planes overseas to test the market. Ford's first, and what turned out to be his only, significant overseas aviation activity started in 1929 when a large 5AT model Tri-Motor was exhibited in July at the International Aero Exhibition held at Olympia Gardens in London. Following the exhibition, many demonstration flights were made in England and then the Ford plane was taken on an extensive tour of 21 European countries. During this tour, 325 demonstration flights were made carrying nearly 4,000 passen-

gers and ended with the big Ford plane being displayed in the International Aeronautic Exposition in Paris from November 28 to December 12. During this tour, Ford pilot

Two dismantled Ford Tri-Motors being hoisted aboard ship for transportation to England. Wing tips have been stored separately. (HFM 833.55632.3)

Ford Tri-Motor 5AT-50 at International Aero Exhibition in Olympia Gardens, London, England in 1929. This plane was eventually purchased by the Czechoslovakian Government. (Robert Baron collection)

Leroy Manning had the opportunity to inspect or flight test most European aircraft, and wrote Mayo in August 1929: *"The difficulty here seems to be that our performance is too good, as compared to the German machines and we have a hard time convincing these people that this is a standard machine, and that its performance is genuine."* He ended the letter with: *"The most important thing I have learned is that the Ford ship is a lot better than anything in Europe."*

Two more planes, a 4AT and another 5AT model, were shipped to England in October 1930, and with special permission of the authorities, were registered as G-ABEF and G-ABHF — Edsel Ford and Henry Ford.

Ford hangar at Ford Aerodrome, Yapton, Sussex, Great Britain with 5AT-58 in the foreground and 4AT-61 in flight over the hangar. (Hudek)

These planes, having been partially disassembled for shipment by boat, were re-assembled and flight tested out of Hooton Park Aerodrome, Cheshire. Needing a permanent operating location, Ford officials found and leased an old airfield at Yapton in Sussex, close to a small village coincidentally named Ford. Known as Yapton or Ford Junction Aerodrome, the name was changed to Ford Aerodrome and would continue to be known by that name for many years, even after Ford ceased aviation operations in England.[1]

of an inch thick. Professor Hugo Junkers, who had earlier tried unsuccessfully to arrange an accommodation with Ford in the United States, rightly perceived the Ford Tri-Motor as a threat to his own operations. Junkers also filed suits against Ford in Greece, Czechoslovakia, Germany and Great Britain. The European suits were finally settled in Junkers favor in November 1930, although the suit in Great Britain appears to have failed with the bankruptcy of Junkers' British company.

Sales results were less than overwhelming. The continental tours resulted in sales of four planes in England (one destined for New Guinea), two to CLASSA, the Spanish government airline, one to the Romanian government and one to the Czechoslovakian airline.

Ford personel who took the 5AT model Tri-Motor for extended demonstration trips through 21 European countries. Left to right: LeRoy Manning, J. Parker VanZandt and Carl Wenzel. Manning and Wenzel died later in separate crashes of Ford Tri-Motor planes. (Robert Baron 833.54200)

With the sale of the first plane in Spain, the German airplane manufacturer, Junkers, instituted a lawsuit against Ford claiming infringement on their patented *"wings with a corrugated skin."* Junkers claimed that the corrugated metal skin on the Ford provided strength to the wing structure as covered in their patent. Ford claimed their wing was designed with all the strength in the structure of the wing, not in the metal covering which was only 12/1000th

While many people have pointed to Junkers' legal actions for the lack of Ford's continuing aviation sales efforts in Europe, it was not the determining factor. The excellent performance and construction of Ford planes was well known in international aeronautical circles by 1929. The United States, however, was not part of the International Com-

Postcard featuring the Dagenham Girl Pipers from the huge Ford plant in Dagenham, England. Performing in front of the Ford Tri-Motor, *Vagabond*. (O'Callaghan collection)

Postcard showing the 5AT model Ford Tri-Motor flying over Rotterdam, The Netherlands during the European demonstration tour. (O'Callaghan collection)

United States had been attempting to join the ICAN for some time, it still faced the task of getting reciprocal agreements with each member country. Germany and England, with fledgling aircraft industries still requiring subsidies, were not anxious to face additional competition (which some felt influenced the outcome of the Junkers' suit). In fact, Great Britain required that operators using aircraft on subsidized airline service, must not only localize purchase of parts and engines, but they must also be of British design. Carried to the extreme, Britain's Imperial Airways purchased two Fokkers from A.V. Roe & Co, the Fokker licensee in England, and after making several inconsequential design modifications, had to then license them as AVRO (A.V.Roe) Tens. In addition, according to Manning's report, every airline in Europe was still heavily subsidized by their government and even then could not show a profit. Obviously, those governments chose to protect their own industries, recognizing the importance of both commercial and military aviation.

mittee of Air Navigation (ICAN) which controlled, in Europe, the development of international air traffic, the regulations governing its operations and the establishment of a common basis for Certificates of Airworthiness. The effect on Ford Motor Company, or any other company of a non-signatory country, was to restrict the licensing of aircraft to private owners for non commercial use. Simply put, American-built planes could not be used commercially in Europe. While the

Ford was not unaware of these barriers for

in October 1929, Mayo wrote Percival Perry, Chairman of Ford Motor Co, Ltd, London, that they originally intended to: *"only show the plane in London and probably could then sell it to some customer who had seen it at the show."* and *"afterward we were of the opinion that it would be a good idea to send this plane on the continental tour, as it would be a great help in adding to the prominence of the Ford Company's name."* Following the tour, with losses mounting in the the United States due to the Depression, Ford tried to charge their affiliates in England and Europe with the expenses of the tour, claiming they were the major beneficiaries of the visit, a claim vigorously denied by Ford of England.

In January of 1932, with the Depression in the United States in full-swing, Edsel Ford wrote Sorensen: *"I would not be sorry if he (Perry) closed up the whole department."* In May, when Edsel Ford directed Sorensen to liquidate the Aviation Department in London as soon as possible, they found Perry had taken a 21 year lease on the Ford Airport at Yapton for $2,500 per annum which only added to Edsel Ford's determination to close the British operation. In Perry's defense, all haste was called for in locating an appropriate airfield in 1929 with arrival of the first Ford plane. After examining nearly 40 sites, Yapton was the only one offering a suitable field with needed facilities coupled with easy access to London and what, at the time, seemed like reasonable lease terms.

The few Ford planes that were purchased for use in the United Kingdom proved useful in World War II. Ford Tri-Motor 5AT-107 is reported to have served with the 271st Squadron of the Royal Air Force in World War II and, unlikely as it seems, rumors persist that it took part in the 1940 evacuation of British troops from the shores of Dunkirk. Ford Tri-Motors 4AT-68 and 5AT-60 served with the Royal Australian Air Force during the war, both being destroyed in the fighting for New Guinea. The remains of the 5AT are owned by the National Museum in Papua, New Guinea awaiting funds for restoration. There are also persistent stories of Ford planes having served in the Philippines early in the war, but no records have been found to give any credibility to these rumors.

Asian Venture

Ford's only other direct international sales effort occurred in February 1930, when a 5AT model was taken to Yokohama, Japan by Ford Pilots Perry Hutton and Edward Hamilton. A letter dated September 10, 1930 from W. C. Cowling, a Ford official in China looking for land for a factory, offers insight as to the conditions experienced in Japan and China. Cowling reported there had been no groundwork laid for the exhibition and demonstration of the plane in Japan and the import permit had only been obtained two days before its arrival. No one had even asked the local Ford Manager for his advice about Japanese interest in the Ford plane.

After a brief tour in Japan, with no commercial interest being shown: *"it was decided as a last resort to send the plane to China."* In the course of demonstrating the plane, it became a major concern that Ford not be drawn into China's internal politics by appearing to favor one side over the other in their civil war. After one bombing raid on Peking, the local press expressed the peoples' concern in finding that 80% of the 33 attacking planes shot down had been imported from the United States. Cowling concluded that they had secured practically no benefit in the plane being over there. This plane was finally sold in July 1931 to Marshal Chang Hsueh-Liang, Mukden, Manchuria who also purchased another 5AT which would eventually become the personal transportation of Madam Chaing Kai-shek, wife of the head of the Chinese Republic. China, able to buy all the planes it needed, was in desperate need of pilots, and Perry Hutton stayed on in China for several years flying for the Marshal. Five additional used Ford planes found their way to China in the 1930s.

Latin America

While over 125 Ford Tri-Motor planes were registered in thirteen different countries in Latin America, only 15 were new planes as Ford never mounted a sales effort south of the United States border. All of the 15 new planes were purchased by Pan American Airways and its partially owned affiliate PANAGRA (Pan American and Grace Lines) for use in their Latin American operations. The used Ford planes were purchased in the mid 1930s when the United States airlines replaced them with the modern Boeing 247s and Douglas DC-2s and DC-3s. Because of the Ford plane's ability to land and take off with large loads in limited spaces,[2] it proved invaluable in providing passenger and freight transportation in the mountainous areas of Latin America where no other large planes could operate. Some Ford Tri-Motors were still in daily operation as late as 1955.

Postcard showing 5AT model Ford Tri-Motor with United States and Mexican registration markings. The United States registration was temporary to allow plane to be ferried to Mexico. While this was a new plane, most Ford Tri-Motors sold in Mexico were used. (O'Callaghan collection)

Notes - Chapter 8

(1) Yapton aerodrome had been built in1918 by German prisoners of war and used as a Training Depot Station for the United States Air Service in World War I. In 1937, it was acquired by the British Air Ministry and turned into a Royal Air Force base. *(page 107)*

(2) The National Air and Space Administration remarked in a 1976 brochure that: *"by today's standards, the Ford Tri-Motor would be classified as a STOL type aircraft like the Harrier jet, that is, a plane capable of 'Short Take Offs and Landings'." (page 110)*

9

THE LINDBERGH CONNECTION

Henry Ford Meets Charles Lindbergh

A United States Navy Curtiss seaplane, backed up by more than sixty Navy ships deployed at 50 mile intervals from Newfoundland to the Azores, crossed the Atlantic Ocean in May 1919. A month later, two British airmen flew a converted Vickers-Vimy bomber from Newfoundland to Ireland and by 1925, dirigibles had crossed the Atlantic several times. But it wasn't until an ex-Air Mail pilot and reserve Captain in the U.S. Army Air Corps flew a single engine plane alone from New York to Paris that the public really awoke to the possibilities of aviation.

In May 1927, Charles A. Lindbergh became the first person to fly alone across the Atlantic Ocean from New York to Paris and in doing so, become the most famous individual in America and probably the civilized world. As a result of that flight and the resultant publicity and pride of the American public, Charles Lindbergh and Henry Ford would meet and develop a lasting friendship.

Most of what has been written about this re-lationship concerns Lindbergh's work at the Ford bomber plant at Willow Run, Michigan, during World War II. Few people realize that this association started nearly 15 years earlier.

The first connection established between Ford and Lindbergh was generated by the news media on June 1, 1927 when Lindbergh was being honored in London following his epic flight. Large headlines in the Detroit News blared: *FORD OFFERS $10,000,000.* The article went on to state that: *"Henry Ford had offered Lindbergh general managership of the aircraft division of the Ford Motor Company and $10,000,000 interest in the Ford airplane enterprises."* The following day, The Detroit Free Press ran a much smaller article: *DENIES OFFER TO LINDBERGH.* Ford sources were quoted: *"Ford was awaiting a quieter day when any personal tribute would have less chance of being misunderstood as a 'wish to share in the thunder'."* In addition, the amount quoted was outlandish. Ten million dollars was nearly the total amount that Ford would spend on his entire aviation venture between 1924 and 1933. Ford sources did not say, however, that Henry Ford was not thinking about offering Lindbergh a position.

It would be another month before Henry Ford and Charles Lindbergh would meet for the

Henry Ford greeting Charles Lindbergh on his arrival at Ford Airport in August 1927. Following his epic New York to Paris flight, Lindbergh undertook a tour visiting all the individual states in the United States. Henry Ford's airport was the only suitable one in the Detroit Metropolitan area at the time. (Hudek 189.4580)

first time. Lindbergh, unannounced, flew into Selfridge Field, Mt. Clemens, Michigan on July 1, 1927 on his way to Ottawa, Canada to help celebrate the 60th anniversary of Canadian Confederation. Lindbergh made

the unannounced stop to see his mother, Evangeline Lindbergh, who was a school teacher in Detroit. Landing at Selfridge Field, he was the guest of Major and Mrs.Thomas Lanphier, an old friend and the base Commandant of Selfridge. The Lanphiers hosted a dinner for him that evening and according to newspaper accounts, Lindbergh's mother, Mr. and Mrs. Henry Ford, Mr. and Mrs. Edsel Ford and Mr. and Mrs. William Mayo, head of Ford aviation, were the only guests in attendance. While there are no records in the Ford archives bearing on this first meeting, and in spite of the earlier denial of a job offer, it is reasonable to speculate that Lindbergh was offered some prominent position with Ford's Airplane Division. Persuading Lindbergh to accept a position with the Ford Motor Company would have been a masterful stroke by Henry Ford. It would have given the Ford Motor Company, whose sales had plunged to a ten year low, suffering from the old fashioned, outdated Model T, a great deal of favorable publicity, and would have also brought the aeronautical talents of Lindbergh to bear on Ford's aviation enterprises.

Henry Ford and Charles Lindbergh probably

Edsel Ford, Charles Lindbergh and Henry Ford pose in the Ford hangar during Lindbergh's August 1927 visit. (HFM 189.4587)

has been widely reported that neither did Lindbergh. In fact Lindbergh, when observed smoking a cigarette at his welcoming banquet in Indianapolis, Indiana in August 1927 stated: *"I do not smoke habitually nor do I drink,"* but in a follow-up question about drinking, he acknowledged to a reporter that he was not drinking water at the many banquet toasts held for him in Europe.

took to each other quite readily, having much in common starting with their heritage of being born in Michigan; Henry Ford in Springwells Township (now Dearborn) in 1863 and Charles Lindbergh in Detroit in 1902. Both were raised on a farm and were mechanically inclined at an early age. Lindbergh had become a U.S. Air Mail pilot in 1926 and Ford was the first private contractor to carry the U.S. airmail with his Ford Air Transportation Service, also in 1926. By 1927, both were men of worldwide fame and held in high esteem by the public and both held great expectations for the future of aviation. They were retiring individuals preferring a rather simple lifestyle and uncomfortable with the adulation of the press while at the same time appreciating and utilizing it to their own ends.

Henry Ford neither drank or smoked and it

Ford and Lindbergh would share one more common bond in 1938. They both would suffer the severe criticism of certain segments of the press and the American Jewish population when they received unsought decorations from Germany. Henry Ford was awarded the Grand Cross of the Supreme Order of the German Eagle in July 1938 for the development of transportation for the average man. With a large investment and many employees in Germany, Ford accepted the award, not in sympathy with the Nazi government, but as a gesture from the German people. (Besides it would probably upset President Franklin Roosevelt with whom he had been feuding over the National Recovery Act.) In November 1938, Lindbergh was invited to a reception and dinner at the American Embassy in Berlin. The American Ambassador hoped Lindbergh's presence would attract Herman Goering. Surprising all in attendance, Goering awarded Lindbergh the Service Cross of the Order of the German Eagle with Star for his services in advancing aviation. Rejecting it would have embarrassed the Ambassador and jeopardized the Ambassador's planned humanitarian negotiations with Herman Goering.[1]

Henry Ford's First Airplane Ride

After Lindbergh's epic flight, the Daniel Guggenheim Fund sponsored a national tour for Lindbergh in his Ryan airplane the *Spirit of St. Louis*, to visit every state in the union, allowing America to see its newest hero. On August 10, 1927, Lindbergh returned to Detroit as part of the national tour, landing his airplane at Ford Airport as Detroit had no other suitable airfield. The welcoming crowd was estimated to be over 75,000 at and around the airport, and Henry and Edsel Ford were the first to greet him when he stepped from his plane. While the Ford organization was heavily involved with aviation by this time, Henry Ford had never flown. At the welcoming banquet that evening, Mrs. Lindbergh was reported to have remarked to Henry Ford: *"that it would be a fine thing for some pilot to take him up for his first air ride."* She probably made the same comment to her son, for the next day, Lindbergh relates in his book The War Journals of Charles Lindbergh that he offered Henry Ford a ride in *The Spirit of St. Louis*. When Ford unexpectedly accepted: *"he had to sit crouched*

up on the arm of my seat in anything but a comfortable position." As the Ford News (September 1, 1927) related: *"Mr. Ford's first airplane ride was not so comfortable for the temporary seat was not only narrow but somewhat higher than Lindbergh's so that the passenger was forced to bend his head down to keep it from contact with the roof of the cabin. He rode, as it were, on the arm of Lindbergh's chair."* The trip was a ten minute flight over Detroit covering Fair Lane, Ford's home, and the mighty Fordson plant[2] on the Rouge river. (The Fordson plant was laying idle at the time while the new Model A car was being developed.) Contrary to many articles claiming that Henry Ford did not like to fly, the only time he has been quoted on the subject was after flying in the *Spirit of*

Henry Ford departing the *Spirit of St. Louis* after his first airplane ride provided by Charles Lindbergh. Edsel Ford was the next to ride and it was also his first airplane ride. (HFM 833.49739)

Lindbergh's plane *Spirit of St. Louis* and the Ford Flivver housed in the Ford hangar during Lindbergh's visit. (Edward Hebb)

St. Louis:"It was great," he replied, smiling and jumping to the ground. *"There was absolutely nothing to it. You see how easy it looks. Well, when you are riding in a plane, it's just that easy."* Detroit Evening Times (August 12, 1927).

Lindbergh had not only given Henry Ford his first airplane ride, but also gave him the distinction of being the first person to ride in the *Spirit of St. Louis* since his Paris trip. Edsel Ford was next to go up with Lindbergh and it was also his first trip in an airplane. (Lindbergh's third and last passenger while in Dearborn was his mother.) While waiting for a board and pillow to be rigged in the *Spirit of St. Louis* for Ford to sit on, Lindbergh was invited to fly Ford's little single seat Flivver plane, the only pilot other than Harry Brooks, Ford's chief test pilot, to do so. Later that same day, Henry and Edsel

Ford took Lindbergh aloft in one of his Tri-Motor airplanes, piloted by Brooks.[3] That night, Lindbergh and Major Lanphier were Ford's overnight guests at Fair Lane.

Later that year, Henry Ford presented Mrs. Lindbergh with a new Ford. In November, Lindbergh was again in Michigan, flying with Major Lanphier from Selfridge Field to Ford Airport for lunch with the Fords. It is probable that on this trip Lindbergh, Lanphier and several businessmen from St. Louis tried to interest Henry Ford in an air service between St. Louis and New York. It was something Lindbergh and Lanphier had discussed prior to Lindbergh's Paris trip and they now felt the time was ripe. Ford however advised them that the Ford Air Transportation Service was a demonstration line and he was only interested in manufacturing airplanes.

Four aviation enthusiasts meet at Ford Airport in November 1927. Reading left to right: Harry Brooks, Ford pilot, Major Thomas Lanphier, Commander, 1st Fighter Squadron, Selfridge Field, William Mayo, head of Ford Aviation, and Charles Lindbergh. (Hudek B.60248)

The Mexican Trip

Lindbergh flew to Mexico in December 1927, starting his goodwill tour of Latin America. It was on this trip that Lindbergh met his future bride, Anne Morrow, daughter of Dwight Morrow, the U.S. Ambassador to Mexico. Ambassador Morrow extended an invitation to Lindbergh's mother to spend Christmas with her son in Mexico City. Unfortunately, she could not accept Ambassador Morrow's invitation as she was a school teacher and would be unable to get back to Detroit in time for the start of classes. Hearing of the problem, Bill Stout advised Henry Ford, who had his pilots, Harry Books and Harry Russell, fly her, along with Mr. and Mrs. William Stout to Mexico City in one of

his Tri-Motor planes. While in Mexico, Lindbergh flew the Ford Tri-Motor on a number of occasions and Harry Russell, co-pilot and a skilled airplane mechanic, tuned up the *Spirit of St. Louis* for Lindbergh's trip further south. The trip itself was unusual for the times with eight stops covering over 2,000 miles each way. While the trip down took only four days, the trip back took six days as a result of severe snow storms in the midwest. Wherever they landed, the Ford plane and Mrs. Lindbergh drew rousing crowds.

Charles Lindbergh was with Edsel Ford in April 1928 at the Detroit Aircraft Show. In June, he stayed with Edsel Ford during the National Air Tour and in August was again back at Ford Airport visiting Henry Ford.

Between 1929 and 1939, usually during visits to his mother, Lindbergh and his wife visited with the Fords on a number of occasions, several as their overnight guests.

Lindbergh and Lanphier, who had left the Army Air Corps in March 1928, were hired as consultants for the newly formed consortium for a coast-to-coast air-rail service. The Transcontinental Air Transport (TAT, a forerunner of TWA) and the Pennsylvania and Santa Fe Railroads had joined to provide rail service by night and air service by day between New York and Los Angeles to save time on transcontinental flights. One of Lindbergh's first acts was to recommend the purchase of Ford Tri-Motor planes. While friendship for Ford might have played a very small part, the performance of the Ford plane was the deciding factor, for Lindbergh was sold on the safety and reliability of the Ford Tri-Motor.

World War II

By 1939, Lindbergh, having traveled extensively in Germany, was active in the America First Committee attempting to keep America out of the war in Europe. On several occasions through 1940, he visited Henry Ford to enlist his support as Ford's own pacifist views on America's involvement were well known. Once the United States was committed, however, both did all in their power to assist the war effort.

Prior to the war, Henry Ford and Charles Lindbergh had both earned President Roosevelt's enmity. Henry Ford, while initially supporting Roosevelt's programs for recovery, could not abide the National Industrial Recovery Act. Symbolized by the Blue Eagle emblem and introduced in 1933, Ford felt it effectively fixed prices and production, dictated minimum pay and maximum hours and recognized unions. Ford met or exceeded all requirements of the Act but refused to sign it stating that the law did not require that you sign, only that you obey. Ford, as well as the other auto manufacturers who did sign, saw the Act as a potential disaster.

Charles Lindbergh had publicly condemned another of the administration's actions in 1934 when Roosevelt, for political reasons, abruptly canceled all commercial air mail contracts. He assigned the task of flying the mail to Army pilots with tragic results. Untrained in night flying and equipped with inadequate planes, twelve of them died in crashes in the seventy-seven days they were in operation. Also, in April 1941, because of Lindbergh's very public and vocal campaigning to keep American from becoming involved in the European war, Roosevelt called him a *copperhead*, a Civil War term denoting a Northerner who sympathized with the South. In other words, he was a traitor. As a result, Lindbergh, in view of what his Commander-in-Chief had publicly said of him, immediately resigned his Army Air Force

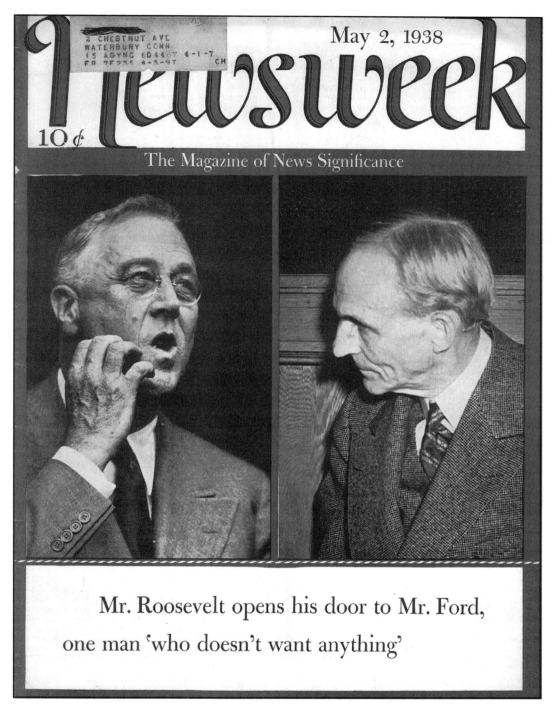

Mr. Roosevelt opens his door to Mr. Ford, one man 'who doesn't want anything'

Newsweek, May 2, 1938. President Roosevelt invited Henry Ford to lunch in an attempt to overcome Ford's objections to the National Recovery Act (NRA). Ford infuriated Roosevelt by not signing saying the law required him to obey the act, not to sign it. Commenting on his unexpected acceptance of the President's luncheon invitation Ford said: *"I am going to give the President a chance to look at somebody who doesn't want anything. I shall not give my advice."*

commission and they would not re-instate him after war was declared. In addition, the aviation industry refused to hire Lindbergh due to the potential, and probably real, political repercussions from the Roosevelt Administration.[4]

Lindbergh wrote Henry Ford offering any aid or advice that might be useful in Ford's aircraft manufacturing. Henry Ford was continually at odds with the meddling Roosevelt administration over the National Industrial Recovery Act, and while Ford obviously thought Lindbergh would be of great value, it is quite conceivable that he also thought he could again irritate Roosevelt by hiring him. Ford offered Lindbergh a job as an advisor on the B-24 bomber project at Willow Run, and Lindbergh and six other pilots were hired when the Willow Run Test Flight Department was organized in late 1941. In his Wartime Journals book, Lindbergh indicates he worked with Ford on aviation problems from April 1942 through June 1942 and as an advisor and test pilot for Ford and other aviation companies until March 1944 when he received permission from the War Department to go to the Pacific Theater of Operations to evaluate the F4U Vought Corsair airplane under combat conditions. (Ford employment records indicate Lindbergh, Ford badge #S9, was hired in November 1941 at a monthly salary of $666.66 and separated July 28, 1942.)

Lindbergh's experience and technical assistance was of great help to the Ford Motor Company in many of its war time aviation projects. One of the more significant ones was high altitude testing described in a later chapter. These and other tests conducted by Charles Lindbergh and other Ford pilots, contributed valuable data on the operation of ignition systems and engine performance at extreme altitudes. In addition, considerable other technical data on high altitude engine performance was obtained. It was some of this Ford experience, coupled with his work with the Chance Vought Company, testing their F4U Corsair fighter plane, that Lindbergh was later able to share with our fighter pilots in the Pacific Theater of Operation.

The Continuing Relationship

In 1940, Lindbergh offered Ford his 1928 Franklin car for the Ford Museum. Lindbergh had been given this car after his flight to Paris by the Franklin Company, as this car was operated by an air-cooled engine and they felt they had benefitted from the fact that his airplane also had an air-cooled engine. This was the only gift Lindbergh had accepted for his personal use as a result of his flight; reasoning the company had, and would continue, to receive advertising benefits.[5] Lindbergh claimed he had his first date with Anne Morrow in that car and later proposed to her in it. Ford accepted the Franklin automobile for the museum and in return presented Lindbergh with a new 1940 Mercury.

Lindbergh's grandfather, Dr. Charles Land, was a prominent dentist in Detroit and had developed and patented many techniques of porcelain dentistry including furnaces for use in their manufacture. In 1941, Lindbergh donated one of Doctor Land's early porcelain furnaces to Henry Ford for his museum. Unfortunately, there is no record of it today.

Henry Ford, in 1942, learning that Lindbergh was looking for a place separate from his house so he and his wife could write without interruptions, gave them a 1935 model Stage Coach trailer he had purchased for his museum. For the next fifteen years, the Lindberghs used this trailer for working on their manuscripts and in covering over 36 states in their travels around America. Lindbergh returned the trailer to the Henry Ford Museum in 1957 where it is currently on display. In returning the trailer he commented that when he protested Mr. Ford's gift in 1942: *"Mr. Ford laughed and said it would be worth more for a museum exhibit after it had been in use."* Ford was no doubt thinking of the Lindbergh connection.

Lindbergh had purchased a new Excelsior motorcyle in 1920 for use while attending college and later when he was learning to fly. Abandoned, the motorcycle was found and restored in 1929 and returned to Lindbergh as a gift in 1931. Because of his frienship with Henry Ford and the favors Ford had rendered, Lindbergh donated this motorcycle to the Henry Ford Museum in 1943 where it is currently on display.

Lindbergh's last connection with the Fords came in 1959, twelve years after Henry Ford's death. In making the movie *The Spirit of St. Louis*, a duplicate of Lindbergh's plane was needed, as the original plane was in the Smithsonian Institution in Washington, DC. James Stewart, who played Lindbergh in the movie, found an original 1927 Ryan Brougham NYP model (New York Paris), that had been built shortly after Lindbergh's flight, in a Denver, Colorado garage. Purchasing it, he had it restored and modified to the original *Spirit of St. Louis* specifications with the sole exception of the addition of a second cockpit required by the Civil Aviation Board. In October 1959, the thirtieth anniversary of the Henry Ford Museum & Greenfield Village, James Stewart sent William Clay Ford, a grandson of Henry Ford, a telegram: *"In view of your museum's outstanding leadership in preserving our American heritage, I would like to offer my airplane, built under the supervision of General Lindbergh for the film Spirit of St. Louis."* Upon learning of the donation, Lindbergh remarked: *"I am, of course, delighted to have it there."* The plane is currently on display in the museum.

The final chapter was written by Lindbergh in 1971 in a letter to the Curator of Transportation of the Henry Ford Museum: *"I have always felt a little embarrassed by the fact that all of my items in the Henry Ford Mu-*

seum are non-Ford (auto, motorcycle, trailer), whereas actually I have been more clearly associated with Ford automobiles through the years than any others. I learned to drive on a 1912 Model T. I had half interest in a Ford Roadster in Missouri when I *was an airmail pilot. For many years, I drove the Mercury Mr. Ford insisted in giving me. We always pulled the trailer with a Ford. Now we have a three year old Falcon wagon, and I am entering my fifty-eighth year of driving Ford cars."*

Notes - Chapter 9

(1) A <u>New York Times</u> article dated January 17, 1960 summarized a manuscript by Colonel Truman Smith, Military Attache in Berlin in 1938, written for the Army Intelligence Division for historical purposes. Smith stated that Ambassador Hugh Wilson used Lindbergh's visit as an inducement to attract Herman Goering to a state dinner so that he, Wilson, could try to obtain Goering's support for assisting Jews who were being forced to flee Germany in a penniless condition. He cites a 1941 letter written by Wilson to Lindbergh: *"Neither you or I had any previous hint the presentation would be made."* Its refusal, the letter adds: *"would have been an act offensive to a guest of the Ambassador of your country." (page 115)*

(2) The Fordson Plant started out as the River Rouge Plant when first built in 1919. In 1925, Springwells Township changed its name to Fordson in tribute to the prominence of the Fordson tractor being built there, and Ford changed the River Rouge Plant name to Fordson. In 1929, Fordson and the Village of Dearborn merged taking the name Dearborn and Ford changed the Fordson plant name to the Rouge Plant. *(page 115)*

(3) In July 1936, Henry Ford would have his third and last ride in an airplane, a Douglas DC-3. It was the plane that had replaced the Ford Tri-Motor in airline passenger service and had been sent to Detroit by C. R. Smith, President of American Airlines. *(page 116)*

(4) Both men were to be vindicated. The National Industrial Recovery Act was overturned by the Supreme Court and Lindbergh was reinstated and promoted to the rank of Brigadier General in the United States Air Force Reserve in February 1954 by President Dwight Eisenhower. *(page 120)*

(5) Lindbergh was sent innumerable gifts from an adulating public, many of which are stored in a warehouse of the Missouri Historical Society. However, according to Leslie Henry, former Transportation Curator of the Henry Ford Museum, who had a number of conversations with Lindbergh, this was the only gift he personally accepted and used. *(page 120)*

10

EXPERIMENTAL PLANES

Henry Ford had expressed his belief on many occasions that larger planes capable of carrying 100 passengers would be needed before aviation could be a commercial success. At the same time he felt there was great potential for the individual aircraft market. As a result, he allowed considerable leeway to his engineers in experimenting, not only with all sorts of engine combinations for the big Tri-Motor planes looking for improved power and performance, but also in developing a number of other very distinct aircraft as the following list indicates:

1926	Single seat, low wing Flivver (# 1) with Anzani engine
1927	Single seat, low wing Flivver (# 2) with Ford engine
1927	Single seat, low wing Flivver (# 3) with Ford engine
1945	Single seat, low wing Flivver (# 4) with Ford engine
1927	Two seat, twin engine amphibian
1927	Five seat, single engine, high-wing monoplane
1929	Single engine freighter - 8AT (modified 5AT)
1930	Tri-motor with outboard engines buried in wings - 5AT-80
1931	Army Bomber XB906 (modified 5AT)
1932	32 passenger, low wing Tri-Motor transport - 14AT
1932	14 passenger, low wing twin-engine transport (model) -15AT
1936	Two seat, flying wing - 15P

Flivver #1

Lawrence Sperry, son of the inventor of the gyroscope, was well known for his aerial exploits and his development of aviation instruments to aid in the safety of flying. He had also started his own airplane company, building a small airplane he referred to as a Flivver.

In 1923, he landed his Flivver, a one seat biplane called the *Sperry Messenger*, on the lawn at Fair Lane, Henry Ford's estate in Dearborn, Michigan. In a <u>Detroit News</u> (October 16, 1923) interview, Sperry related how Edsel Ford was intrigued with the potential of a small plane. He quoted Edsel Ford as commenting: *"that when they first sold their*

Henry ford revealing his first one-man Flivver airplane to newsmen on July 30, 1926. (John Bluth collection)

cars they were obliged to push them with people who got no practical use of them, but who had the pioneer spirit, and despite the necessity of lying under those cars most of the time, they bought and made them run. We ought to be able to sell 'airplane flivvers' to the same type of individuals — to pioneers who are going to break unbroken ground and fly, despite all obstacles." Henry Ford, Sperry noted, was more interested in the engine than the airplane, estimating he could build a similar engine for $50.

Less than two years later the <u>New York Times</u> (April 19, 1925) reported that the Fords intended to *"Flivverize the air"* and that: *"several designs had been drawn on paper and at least one of them had been set up as a model to see how it would look."* But they went on to report: *"the small Ford plane must*

Charles Lindbergh ready to take off in the Ford Flivver during his August 1927 visit. He and Harry Brooks were the only two people to fly the plane. This plane currently hangs in the main hall of the Henry Ford Museum in Dearborn, Michigan. (Hudek 0.996)

wait the development of the Ford aircraft engine." The Sample Case, a commercial travelers' magazine, was quick to pick up on the idea of a small personal plane. In its July 1925 issue, it indulged in what they called: *"wild speculating on a broad scale"* that *"just as Henry Ford's Model T had enabled the traveling salesman to contact 5 to 10 towns a day, within a few years planes would enable him to contact up to 20 towns a day."*

A small plane had been glimpsed in test flights around Ford Airport in the summer of 1926 (it was first flown June 8th), but like many of Ford's projects, confirmation was difficult to come by until Henry Ford was ready to do so. It was not made official until July 30, 1926 on the occasion of Henry Ford's usual birthday interview with newspapermen. First publicly demonstrated at the start of the 2nd National Air Tour on August 7, 1926, the Flivver generated a great deal of press attention and while most of the press and public hailed this plane as the Model T of the air, a plane for the masses, the Grand Rapids Press, (Michigan) (July 31, 1925) was less elated stating: *"A sturdy little Ford plane, put on the market, say at $498 fully equipped with standard gear shift and balloon tires, would be a national menace. The longer American aviation remains in the hands of the large common carrier, instead of the pri-*

vate pleasure adventurer, the better all around." Ford publicly denied any intentions of mass producing the Flivver.

The plane was designed by Otto Koppen, a recent graduate of Massachusetts Institute of Technology and built by Jim Lynch, an out-

Harry Brooks flying the Flivver around the Navy's airship Los Angeles. Very unusual for someone who was considered a very careful, professional pilot. (Hudek 189.3769)

standing wood worker who had built racing boats for Edsel Ford. In later years, Koppen related how the dimensions of the airplane was determined when Henry Ford told him he wanted a plane that would fit inside of his office. The plane was a fabric covered wooden frame 16 feet long with a wing span of 21 feet 9 inches, weighing 320 pounds. For ease of ground transportation, the wings were held on by two bolts on either side.

While the plane was powered by a three cylinder Anzani air-cooled engine developing 35 hp and a top speed of 85 mph, Ford had announced at the Flivver's unveiling that Ford engineers were already working on a two cylinder replacement engine. In any event, it was a quick, nimble craft as demonstrated in Ford motion picture film of the period showing it getting off the ground in about three seconds. The plane was flown only by Harry Brooks, Henry Ford's favorite pilot, and once by Charles Lindbergh on the occasion of his visit to Ford Airport in August 1927. Lindbergh was so impressed that he was quoted as saying: *"Well, that's great! That gives you a real sensation of flying that you can't get in one of the larger planes."* The plane was completely restored in 1981 by the Detroit Institute of Aeronautics and currently hangs in the Henry Ford Museum in Dearborn, Michigan.

Flivver #2

A close scrutiny of this plane, versus the first Flivver, reveals marked differences. The fuselage is different and it carries the new Ford-designed two cylinder engine. This plane could actually be the first Flivver modified but in any event, was apparently only a test bed for the new Ford two-cylinder engine. It was displayed in Ford's New York showroom and pictured in the <u>Ford News</u> (January 22, 1927). All that is known about this plane is contained in that <u>Ford News</u> article: *"the plane weighed 350 pounds* (about the same weight as #1) *with a new Ford-built two cylinder engine and carried sufficient fuel for two and a half hours flight."* There is no record of it having ever flown or having been licensed.

Second Flivver airplane. Note the new Ford two cylinder engine and high pilot headrest among several of the differences from the first Flivver plane. (Hudek 189.8147)

Harry Brooks on beach in Titusville, Florida beside the third Flivver in which he set the small plane long distance record before being forced down for lack of gas. On taking off four days later, he crashed into the ocean and his body was never recovered. (John Bluth collection)

Flivver #3

With the aviation craze generated by Lindbergh's historic flight over the Atlantic Ocean in 1927, everyone wanted to break records, and it was undoubtedly the motivating factor in building Flivver #3. This plane was designed and built to break the world's existing light plane distance record of 870 miles. Otto Koppen also designed this plane, with substantial input from Harry Brooks, and it was introduced to the public at Ford Airport on the ocassion of the start of the Gordon Bennett International Balloon Race September 10, 1927. To the casual observer Flivvers #1, #2 and #3 seem similar but #3 was substantially different. It was a larger plane with a fabric covered steel frame and powered by the new Ford engine. The engine, apparently comprised of two of the

Wreckage of the Ford Flivver recovered after Harry Brooks crashed into the Atlantic Ocean. It is hard to accept that this wreckage was supposedly reconstructed into the Flivver airplane Brooks was flying. (HFM 188.8150)

Wright Whirlwind engine cylinders as used in the Tri-Motor, developed 29 hp with a top speed of 90 mph. The plane was 16 feet 6 inches long with a wing span of 25 feet and weighed 550 pounds empty. The magazine <u>Aviation</u> (February 27, 1928) stated: *"it has carried more than its own weight and carries the same load in proportion to its lifting surface as the most efficient large plane."*

On January 25, 1928, Harry Brooks took off from Ford Airport, Dearborn, Michigan in Flivver #3, heading for Miami, Florida in an attempt to break the world Class "C" light plane record. Nine hours and 500 miles later, he was forced down in Emma, North Carolina by bad weather and icing. While he hadn't set a world's record, he had bettered the U.S. record of 472 miles. On February 21, 1928, Brooks tried again, leaving Ford Airport once again headed for Miami, Florida and a gala reception by Henry Ford and many Ford dealers on hand to welcome him. He managed to fly non-stop to Titusville, Florida, where he was forced to land on the beach due to a fuel line leak. While falling

short of his Miami Beach destination, he did set a new world's record certified at 972 miles. This was quite a feat considering this flight was in an open cockpit in the middle of the winter. Unfortunately, four days later as he attempted to complete his journey to Miami, he crashed in the Atlantic ocean and although the plane wreckage was recovered, his body was never found.

Henry Ford was very fond of Harry Brooks and his untimely death at age 25 was a personal blow. While there has been much speculation as to the cause of the crash, nothing definitive was ever established, and notwithstanding Henry Ford's remarks that the accident would not deter efforts towards developing small airplanes for everyday use, it did end Ford's experiments with small planes until 1935. Brook's death did not, however, have anything to do with Henry Ford quitting aviation, as so many writers have claimed, as production of the big Ford Tri-Motors continued expanding until the Depression hit in late 1929.

Flivver #4

In researching the Ford Flivvers, records were discovered that indicated there was a fourth Flivver. Accession records in the Henry Ford

Newly discovered Flivver #4. It was reported that Flivver #3 had been rebuilt, but photograph of wreckage strongly indicates a new plane was constructed. (HFM 189.21491)

Museum state: *"It (Flivver #3) was brought back to Dearborn, restored and placed in the Museum."* A later notation in 1951 indicates it was missing from the museum and a marginal notation states: *"Mr. D (undoubtedly Ray Dahlinger, one of Henry Ford's chief aids) had the plane destroyed."* In addition, Al Esper, a Ford engineer states in his 1951 Oral Reminiscences: *"They brought back parts and put them together. I saw it when it was completed, and it looked the same as it did before it was cracked."* He further stated that it was in the museum at the present time (1951). Also, John Dahlinger states, in his 1978 autobiography The Secret Life of Henry Ford: *"After Brooksie died in the plane, it was rebuilt and during the war kept at Ford Airport."* Dahlinger, who claimed to be the illegitimate son of Henry Ford, went on to say that he had flown the rebuilt Flivver with Henry Ford's permission. No Ford records concerning this plane were found, but in subsequent searching through Ford photographs taken in 1945, pictures of a new Flivver were discovered. Previous Ford aviation researchers had never looked beyond the 1930s for Ford airplanes. Shown in the Ford hangar in a photograph dated October 24, 1945, is a picture of a Flivver airplane with several small differences from Flivver #3. Confirmation of the existence of this Flivver #4 was made with the discovery of a Ford Supervi-

sory Bulletin in the Henry Ford Museum archives. Dated November 1, 1945, just eight days after the photograph, it reads: *"FLIVVER PLANE FLYS AGAIN: The historic Ford flivver plane which on February 21, 1928, flew from Dearborn, Michigan to a point near Jacksonville, Florida establishing a light plane non-stop record, recently took to the air again at Ford Airport.....The tiny, two cylinder plane has been completely rebuilt.It will find a permanent haven in the Edison Museum."*

In spite of the above comments indicating that Flivver #3 was rebuilt, it is apparent, in viewing photographs of the wreckage, that a new plane was constructed.

Two seat, twin engine amphibian designed by Bill Stout in April 1927. It was not a successful design. (Hudek 189.4249)

Two Seat Amphibian

With the success of the 4AT model Tri-Motor, Henry Ford apparently softened his attitude towards Bill Stout as a result of the 3AT model fiasco. By April 1927, Stout had finished designing and building an all-metal, two seat, twin engine, tandem wing amphibian that he had been working on since July 1925. The plane was powered by a pair of 4 cylinder Bristol Cherub engines that could never be made to run properly. Taxied once by test pilot Leonard Flo, it hit a bump at 70 mph, bounced ten feet in the air and collapsed the landing gear on impact. One of the engines was salvaged for use in a small one seat vehicle built for Henry Ford's grandsons. All that is known about this plane is in the notes of Robert Baron and the <u>Oral Reminiscences</u> of Bill Stout and Harold Hicks, Chief Design Engineer of the Airplane Division.

of 3,700 pounds. It was a serious attempt by Ford to enter the executive/recreation market as evidenced by an article in the <u>Ford News</u> (June 22, 1927) and Mayo's interview with <u>Automotive Industries</u> (August 20, 1927): *"The Stout Metal Airplane Division of Ford Motor Co. will start production of a single-engined, five-passenger, closed-cabin, all-metal monoplane."* Unfortunately, it didn't fly very well. The engine was not placed far enough forward to give it proper balance and the pilot, Eddie Hamilton, declared after the test flight: *"I think you should run a band saw through it before you kill*

Five seat executive plane designed by Bill Stout. It flew so poorly that the test pilot said a band saw should be run through it before it killed somebody. (Hudek 189.4652)

sion. There is no record of it having received an experimental registration from the Department of Commerce.

Five Seat Executive Monoplane

This plane, also designed by Stout, was being built at the same time as the two seat, twin engine amphibian. It was an all-metal, five seat high wing monoplane powered by a Wright Whirlwind J-5 engine of 225 hp with a wingspan of 45 feet and a gross weight

somebody." License number X-1085 was issued August 1, 1927 and canceled February 15, 1929. No other information has been found on this plane.

Single Engine Freighter - 8AT

At the peak of Ford production in 1929, Ford was looking ahead to expand, and the single-engine 8AT freighter for commercial use and the XB906 bomber for the military were attempts to exploit these markets. On July 30,

With the advent of more powerful engines, the Tri-Motor could fly on one. This 8AT model equipped with a Hispano-Suiza engine was designed for freight where an appearance of safety with three engines wasn't necessary. (Hudek 189.8615)

1929, Ford first flew the 8AT with a single Pratt & Whitney Hornet engine in an attempt to develop a plane for pure freight use. The original 4AT Tri-Motor had been developed with three motors to increase its dependability and convince the public of the safety of air travel. With the greatly increased power and reliability available with the new engines, a single engine plane became feasible especially in carrying freight where the image of safety was not a concern. Horsepower was no longer a problem. The three Wright J-4 engines on the first 4ATs were rated at 200 hp each for a total of 600 hp while the final single engine tested in the 8AT, a Wright Cyclone, was rated at 700 hp.

For almost five years, Ford experimented with about eight different engines, according to Bob Baron, finally introducing the 8AT to the public on April 9, 1931 with a 600 hp

Hispano-Suiza engine. The 8AT had the same fuselage, tail and wing of the standard 5AT airframe. With two less engines, the drag was reduced, making the plane slightly faster and less costly to maintain. Ford was serious about their new plane, advertising it in August 1931 with the caption: *"Ford Express — The time has come for freight to fly!"* This was the only 8AT model built and was sold in May 1934 to Pacific Alaska Airways, a subsidiary of Pan American Airways. In 1941, Avianca of Columbia wrote the factory requesting information on how to convert the plane to a tri-motor configuration.

5AT-80 with experimental engine configuration. Position of the engines affected lift of the wing and did not offer any improvement over the standard configuration. It was rebuilt and sold as a conventional 5AT model. (Hudek 189.7721)

As all aviation plans and drawings had been put in storage and there were no Airplane Division engineers left, there was no one to answer their question.

Tri-Motor With Engines In Wings - 5AT-80

Rare photograph of wind tunnel test of the 5AT-80 in the University of Detroit's wind tunnel. William Mayo is lower right. (O'Callaghan collection)

This adaptation of a standard 5AT airframe included two 300 hp Wright J-6 engines buried in the wings and one 575 hp Wright Cyclone in the nose. While top speed improved marginally, it was offset by an increase in the landing speed. In addition, according to Bob Baron, it caused too much turbulence and blanked out too much of the lifting area of the wing. As a result it was reconverted to a standard Tri-Motor and sold to National Air Transport.

Army Bomber XB906

While Ford had sold 22 planes to the Army, Navy and Marines, they were all for transport use. In May 1930, Ford sent a plane to the Army maneuvers in Sacramento, California. Army officers, under the impression that Ford was sending a plane that had been converted into a bomber, were quite disappointed to see a standard Ford plane and strongly implied that: *"Ford Motor Company should build a bomber for their approval."* Ford, interested in participating in this segment of the military market responded with the XB906. It was a highly modified 5AT-D and was flight tested on April 7, 1931. It was 505 pounds heavier, with a top speed of 156 mph (6 mph faster) and could fly to 20,000 feet vs. 16,100 feet for the standard 5AT-D. It had a rounded, more modern tail and, unlike all other Ford

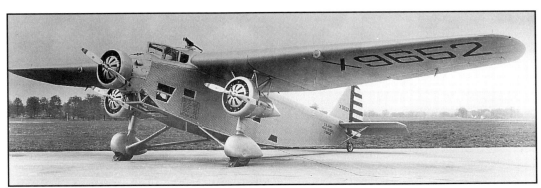

XB906 was an attempt to obtain U.S. Army combat airplane orders. The Army wasn't impressed and the plane later crashed, killing two Ford employees. (Hudek 833.56183.1)

Tri-Motor planes, all control cables were located inside the plane. The Army Air Corp tested the plane in July 1931 at Wright Field, Ohio and in replying to a Ford query summed up their four page critique as follows: *"While the airplane had some excellent bombing characteristics, these were offset by a large margin due to the lack of rearward vision, inadequate angles of fire for machine guns and inherently poor aerodynamic qualities."* In returning the plane to Ford, a storm was encountered at 12,000 feet. The plane was first hit with a strong up current and in trying to bring the plane under control the flying speed fell to 80 mph. Then it was hit with a down draft and before the plane was righted, a speed of 205 mph to 210 mph was noted. Two comments on this trip worth mentioning are in a memo submitted to Mayo by S. H. Morse, a Ford engineer who was a passenger: *"Lt. Berry* (the Army pilot) *informed*

Artist rendering of 10AT model equipped with four Pratt & Whitney Hornet engines. With different engines, this model evolved into the 12AT and finally the 14AT. (Hudek 189.8393)

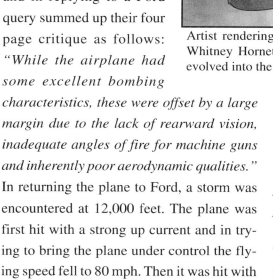

the writer that he was prepared to leave the ship when it reached the high air speed of 205 mph because he thought that something would give way." and *"The structure of the plane, in the writer's estimation was no doubt put to a very severe test during this flight."*

This plane crashed September 19, 1931, killing Ford's chief test pilot Leroy Manning and his flight mechanic Lycurgus Garriot. The only official comment on the crash came from Mayo who said the crash was apparently the result of a motor explosion while the ship was in a power dive. Eyewitnesses reported seeing the right wing lift up and

14AT — Henry Ford's 100 passenger dream. A 32 passenger plane that cost over $1,000,000. While it never flew, many innovative assembly and manufacturing techniques were developed. (Hudek 833.56854.7)

separate from the fuselage, causing the plane to barrel-roll into the ground.

An interesting side note was found on the reverse of one of the photographs of the wreck: *"One half hour after the crash, not one speck of material could be found. Ford's Ray Sherman cleared everything away."* The remains of the plane were taken to the Ford hangar and extensively photographed.

32 Passenger 14AT

Henry Ford had been convinced, even before his acquisition of the Stout Metal Airplane Company, that in order for aviation to be profitable, larger planes had to be developed: planes capable of carrying at least 100 people. In July 1927, the New York Times quoted Mayo: *"I have devoted more than two years to the designing of a 100 passenger plane and a 1,000 horsepower air-cooled radial engine."* This, at a time when few planes even carried ten passengers. However, with the existing state of aircraft and engine design at the time, this larger plane was not possible.

By 1929, with the success of his 4AT and 5AT model Tri-Motors and discussions with Charles Lindbergh and other aviation pioneers, Ford was convinced the time was ripe for a bigger plane. Bill Stout relates that when Henry Ford discussed the development of this large plane, he cautioned Ford that it might be wiser to build a smaller plane first. Ford replied: *"No, I would rather build a big*

plane and learn something, even if it didn't fly, than to build a smaller one that worked perfectly and not learn anything."

In late 1929, the 10AT was designed, a 32 passenger plane to be powered by four of the new Pratt & Whitney 575 hp Hornet engines developing a total of 2,300 hp. One engine was buried in each wing and two engines, a pusher and a tractor, were mounted on a pedestal on top of the center section of the plane. A later design, designated 12AT, featured a single 1000 hp Hispano-Suiza engine mounted on top as a tractor with two 575 hp Hornets in the wings. By early 1930, the final engine selection was made and the plane was designated 14AT. The 1000 hp Hispano-Suiza center engine was matched with two 650 hp Hispano-Suiza engines mounted in each wing. (In all cases, the fuselage, tail and wings of the 10AT, 12AT and 14AT were the same. The model numbers changed as the different engine combinations changed.) Hicks stated in his Oral Reminiscences that the switch to the heavy water-cooled Hispano-Suiza engines reduced the payload by 2,700 pounds and caused the Department of Commerce to reduce the authorized passenger capacity to 10. A review of the Ford Motor Company relations with Pratt & Whitney prepared for Henry Ford II in 1959, stated Henry Ford became displeased because Bill Mayo, Chief Engineer for Ford and running the Aircraft Division, was also a director at Pratt & Whitney. Ford apparently felt there was a conflict of interest even

The only known photograph of the 14AT with landing gear extended nearly 48 inches in take-off mode. When airborne, the wheels retract into the wheel pants. (Ed Johnson collection)

though he had agreed, when Mayo was hired, that he could retain outside interests. He resolved the problem by ordering the switch to the Hispano-Suiza engines even though it greatly diminished the capacity of the planned aircraft. Harold Hicks claimed that Henry Ford had been displeased with Mayo for some time, so the Pratt & Whitney situation probably gave Henry Ford the opportunity to express his displeasure.

This plane was to: *"rival the most luxurious forms of surface transportation"* according to <u>Aero Digest</u> (April 1932). They went on to relate that the passenger compartments would be like Pullman cars with sections on either side of a center aisle. Each section (8'11" x 6'2") would have two facing double seats being convertible into lower sleeping berths. Upper berths would be stored at air depots so no added weight would have to be carried on daytime flights. There was to be a smoking compartment, two lavatories and a galley with call buttons located in each compartment. Further: *"Cabin interiors are fur-*

nished in harmonious color schemes. The seat cushion is constructed of rubber inflated with air to give utmost passenger comfort."

In testing the engines, the 1,000 hp Hispano-Suiza engine mounted on a pedestal on the top of the plane caused considerable difficulty as it could not be kept running. According to Baron, the difficulty was resolved when a Hispano-Suiza representative determined that this tractor engine had been designed as a pusher engine for the 1929 Schneider Racing Cup and the carburetor floats only needed adjustments. These three engines would consume a total of 121 gallons of gas per hour. A unique feature of this plane was the semi-retractable landing gear. The wheels were extended 48 inches for take off and then retracted in flight. When at the gate, the wheels were retracted into the housings, lowering the plane's doorsill close to the ground for passenger access without the aid of a ramp. With the wheels fully extended, Baron said: *"it reminded one of a giant monster ready to leap into the air."*

Specifications of the plane were as follows:

Wing Span   110 feet

Length   80 feet 10 inches

Height (wheels retracted)

           19 feet 6 inches

Height (wheels extended)

           23 feet 7 inches

Gas capacity   500 gallons

Cruising speed   150 mph

According to Baron, the plane never flew and total taxiing distance was less than a half mile. In checking Ford records for information on an unrelated Tri-Motor accident, Baron states he came across a memo stating the cost of the 14AT had reached $1,044,000. The memo was dated before any of the components had been assembled. One of the reasons for the enormous expense was that parts for three planes were fabricated to save future costs, but only one was ever assembled. It was a serious attempt by Ford to build a larger plane as his advertising proclaimed in March 1932: *"When Larger Planes Fly - Larger Ford planes will lead the way."*

In June 1933, Ford requested the Department of Commerce to cancel the license as the plane was being dismantled. The only thing salvaged was the 1000 hp center engine which was mounted on a pedestal and was used for many years on the airport test track to simulate gusty wind conditions as test cars passed by.

Some Ford engineers believed that if the original 10AT with the four air-cooled Pratt & Whitney Hornet engines had been developed, Ford would have been years ahead of other airplane manufacturers.

**Low Wing Passenger 15AT
(Wind Tunnel Model)**

The 15AT design was a low wing monoplane with a length of 51 feet 6 inches, a wing span of 80 feet with a gross weight of 13,340 pounds and passenger capacity for 14 people. It was to have a fully retractable landing gear and be powered by two Curtiss Wright V-1650 engines of 720 hp each, with a projected top speed of 215 mph.

Drawings and a wind tunnel model of the

Wind tunnel model of 15AT in March 1932. Designed about the same time as the DC-1, the forerunner of the famous Douglas DC-3. By now, Henry Ford had decided to quit aviation much to the relief of other airplane manufacturers. (Hudek)

Another Ford Tri-Motor that was never built. (HFM 189.10355)

Design model of 15P (September 1934)
(Hudek 188.11054 - top & 188.11050 -
bottom)

15AT had been prepared by August 1932, and according to Hicks it was: *"almost a dead ringer for the DC-3."* Final design of the DC-1, the prototype of the Douglas DC-3 was also finalized at the same time. The DC-1 first flew in June 1933, and according to a Popular Aviation magazine article in April 1940: *"came into being for several reasons. First, in 1931, Ford discontinued the manufacture of his Tri-Motors."* Henry Ford was busy trying to return his company to a profitable position and regain his former share of the automobile market and the aviation industry's fear of Ford's dominance in aviation was diminished.

Full size mock up of 15P (January 1935)
(Hudek 188.11723)

Flying Wing 15P

By late 1932, the nation was in the depths of a depression and aircraft manufacturing was severely restricted. Production at the Airplane Division of Ford had stopped, although there were several unfinished planes on hand ready for completion to a customer's specifications. While the airport and repair facilities remained operative for many years, Ford was out of the airplane building business. In 1933, Eugene Vidal, Director of the Bureau of Aeronautics for the Department of Commerce, was convinced that the Federal Government, having the responsibility under the Air Commerce Act of 1926, to foster aviation's development, should act to break the industry out of the doldrums. Vidal's thrust was towards development of a low priced, easily operated and maintained airplane for the thousands of young people interested in aviation as a result of their war experiences, model building, Lindbergh's exploits, etc. Vidal had visited with Henry Ford and Ford engineers felt they could produce an automobile engine for such an aircraft for $65.

In November 1933, Vidal issued a press release headlined: *"Plan For Widespread Development Of Private Flying Through Volume Production Of 10,000 Low Priced Airplanes."* The release went on to state that there were 14,000 licensed pilots, 11,000 student pilots and 8,500 licensed aircraft mechanics in the United States and only 7,000

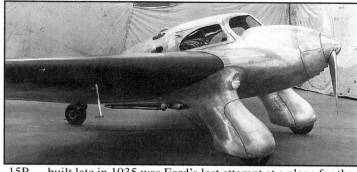

15P — built late in 1935 was Ford's last attempt at a plane for the average person. It was one of the first flying wings, but with a massive six foot propeller and with no tail it was hard to control. (Hudek 188.15927)

licensed aircraft, 600 of which belonged to scheduled airlines. Vidal's goal was an aircraft seating two people, built of steel alloy, fitted with an eight cylinder engine, and equipped with a geared propeller. It would have a landing speed of about 25 miles per hour and cost between $700 and $800. Unfortunately, Vidal's program was ill-timed as few people had $700 or $800 in the mid 1930s to spend so frivolously on something like a small airplane.

Even though Ford's Airplane Division was drawing to a close and the likelihood of mass production was nil, the challenge was too much for Ford to pass up. There still seemed to lurk in Ford's mind the hope of an aerial Flivver for the masses, for in June 1934, Edsel Ford had written Vidal stating they were experimenting with one of their V8 motors for aircraft use.

By September 1934, a design model of a small airplane had been completed, quickly followed by a full size mock up in January 1935. The combination of Ford and aviation still made news, as the New York Times (January 13, 1936) featured a front page article: *"Ford Licenses Experimental Flivver Plane."* In response to the hundreds of let-

Another view of the tailess 15P. (Hudek 188.15928)

ters requesting information on this new plane, the Ford answer was the same — the release was in error and they were not considering building a small plane. Most were referred to the Arrow Aircraft and Motors Corp. of Lincoln, Nebraska. Of the 14 projects authorized under Vidal's program, Arrow's "Sport" Model F, powered by a stock Ford V8 engine, was one of the planes to have received an Approved Type Certificate (ATC) from the Bureau of Air Commerce for a small low-wing monoplane. The Arrow "Sport", as well as all other Ford powered planes, used a standard V8 engine purchased from the local Ford dealer. The high initial cost of airplane engines and replacement parts made the reliable, low cost, Ford V8 a desirable alternative.

15P close up of the souped-up Ford V8 aluminum engine and cockpit. (Hudek 188.15926)

The release of information on Ford's small plane also caused a stir in the Aeronautics Branch of the Department of Commerce as a January 24, 1936 letter from the local inspector states: *"Ford Motor Company was considerably perturbed that the publicity broke before they were ready to make an announcement,"* implying they were the source of the leak to the press. There have been no company records found bearing on the development of this plane. However, oral histories, newspaper accounts and Department of Commerce correspondence build an interesting story of Ford's last fling in civil aviation.

With only four or five men assigned to the airport for handling Tri-Motor repairs, service and any other assigned duties, apparently Edsel Ford had them work on this two seat flying wing, called a bat-wing by some

and given the designation 15P. It is interesting that this was a two seater (side by side) as Bill Stout relates that when Henry Ford approached him with the idea of the original single seat *Flivver* in 1926, he asked Ford: *"How could you teach anyone to fly it without killing him."*

The plane, designed by Harry Karcher, a Massachusetts Institute of Technology graduate, assisted by Gar Evans, a Ford designer/draftsman, was made of steel tubing with the fuselage covered in aluminum alloy and the wings covered with fabric. The following dimensions, which are approximate, were taken from tracings Robert Baron made from the original 1936 drawings by Gar Evans.

Wing span	34 feet
Overall length	14 feet
Height	6 1/2 feet

Harry Russell, the Airport Manager and chief pilot requested License X-999 be assigned to the plane, a reference to the Ford racing car number 999 that Barney Oldfield drove to victory in 1902. It was assigned license number X-999E by the Department of Commerce on November 29, 1935 and subsequently re-registered until January 1, 1937. (The last plane to bear the 999E registration was the Fokker tri-motor that crashed March 31, 1931, killing Knute Rockne, the Notre Dame football coach.)

Power was supplied by a souped up 115 hp Ford V8 engine with a cast aluminum alloy block mounted behind the occupants with the drive shaft passing between them to a large 6 1/2 foot Gardner wooden propeller. It had a standard automotive radiator under the engine, which was retractable into the fuselage. There were two 15 gallon gas tanks mounted in the wings, giving it a cruising range of about 500 miles. The idea of using a nearly standard Ford engine was to allow an owner to obtain parts and repairs at any Ford automobile dealer in the country and be quickly on his way.

The occupants were seated at the center of gravity and longitudinal control was activated by shifting their weight forward or backward. Lateral control was by conventional ailerons, and yawing was controlled by split rudders attached to the trailing edge of the wing tips adjacent to the ailerons. As can be imagined, control of the plane was difficult and the strong torque of the large propeller only made it more so. There was plenty of lift to get off the ground but in spite of everything they could think of, they couldn't control its tendency to turn. After several short flights by Harry Russell, it was involved in an accident and reportedly destroyed.

Aerospace Engineer Vance Jaqua in the May 1998 issue of Contact Magazine analyzed the available data and estimated the plane would have a gross weight of 1,600 pounds and a top speed of 120 mph. His analysis was: *"Could it fly? Of course! The question was; could it be made to fly well?"*

The plane had not been destroyed as rumored. In 1941 Emil Zoerlin, another Ford engineer, states that Henry Ford told him to: *"attempt to make a combination helicopter and standard plane out of it."* This was at the height of the national craze over the Pitcairn Autogyro. The Autogyro was the forerunner of the helicopter and generated reams of media attention whenever and wherever it appeared. While this undoubtedly influenced Ford, it was no sudden whim, for in 1928, L. S. Sheldrick, a Ford engineer, states Henry Ford had them lay out: *"opposed piston engines with multiple crankshafts, which drove propellers that would act in the horizontal direction as well as propellers in the vertical direction."* Also, in a 1928 interview with the New York Times, Ford was quoted as saying: *"A way must be found so that the air-*

plane can descend vertically, so that it won't need a 40 acre field." Ford was undoubtedly aware of the first true Autogyro which had been developed and test flown in 1923. The Autogyro had to remain in motion, unlike the helicopter developed in the 1940s, which could hover motionlessly. The Detroit Free Press (March 10, 1941) reported Henry Ford saying: *"We've been experimenting with a two seater that we expect to put on the market ultimately. It probably will combine features of the ordinary airplane and the 'Gyro' type ship, permitting it to land or take off in* *a small area. The ship will be powered with a motor of 300 hp, built horizontally into the wing. The body will be made of plastics."* A special 10 cylinder engine (5 cylinders opposed) was developed and three engines were actually produced. After much experimenting and in spite of Ford's insistence, the engineers could not make the conversion work and the plane never got off the ground. It wasn't until Charles Lindbergh saw the plane, however, and agreed with the Ford engineers that the plane could not fly that Henry Ford finally let the project die.

11

WILLIAM STOUT, WILLIAM MAYO AND HARRY BROOKS

No discussion of Ford and aviation would be complete without a brief biography of several of the men close to the Fords and their ventures into early aviation. First, there is Bill Stout who never claimed he designed the 4AT model Ford Tri-Motor. Stout did claim: *"In my opinion, the greatest single thing I accomplished for aviation was getting Mr. Ford interested in it.— From that moment on, Wall Street and the country began to take aviation seriously."* Next is Bill Mayo who had the title of Chief Engineer when no one in the company had a title and literally ran the Ford Airplane Division along with a host of other Ford responsibilities. And finally, Harry Brooks, a young man who was a superb pilot and who Henry Ford took an immense interest in, treating him almost like a son.

William Bushnell Stout (1880 - 1956)

William Stout, born in Quincy, Illinois, had an engaging personality and was an innovative inventor, designer, promoter and most of all the consummate salesman. Although he attended the University of Minnesota, he left in his senior year due to severe eye problems. With a fascination for aviation, he covered air meets for the <u>Chicago Tribune</u>,

William Bushnell Stout, May 1929. (Hudek 189.6320)

founded the Model Aero Club of Illinois and was the first editor of the aviation magazine <u>Aerial Age</u>. Limited as it was, this aviation experience was more than most people possessed and as a result, he was selected by Packard Motor Car Company to take charge of their new aircraft division. In 1917, Stout was placed in charge of the Packard's production of the World War I *Liberty* engine. As a result of these efforts, he was called to Washington as a Technical Advisor to the U.S. Aircraft Board during War I. Following the war, with the backing of R. L. Stranahan,

Stout obtained Ford Tri-Motor plans and related data from Henry Ford II in 1954 and used them to design this "Stout Bushmaster", which was built by Hayden Aircraft Corp. Although upwards of one thousand planes were projected, only two were ever built. Note "28 Troop Seats" painted over the door, apparently done in an attempt to sell the plane to the Army. (Hudek)

President of the Champion Spark Plug Company, he formed the Stout Engineering Laboratory which designed and built several small planes, including, in 1922, the first all-metal plane in the United States for the U.S. Navy. Although 14 successful test flights were completed in this all-metal Navy plane by Eddie Stinson, one of the most prominent pilots of the time, the contract was canceled when a Marine pilot crash landed the plane during the final acceptance tests. The Navy plane was followed by the small Air Sedan AS-1 in 1923, which was the first all-metal plane built in the United States for commercial use.

After the fiasco of the ill fated 3AT Tri-Motor airplane built for Henry Ford, Stout became a semi-official public relations representative for Ford's Airplane Division and aviation in general. Robert Walker, Mayo's secretary, afraid that an imminent rupture between Henry Ford and Stout would hurt Stout and aviation, claims to have engineered Stout's leaving by convincing him that he could accomplish more as an outside consultant, free to work on his own projects. In a letter to Mayo, Stout comments on a meeting with Edsel Ford at which it was agreed that he could make more progress at research in a little laboratory of his own without restrictions of any kind. Stout severed all official connections with Ford in March 1930. That same month, after being engaged in aviation most of his life, he soloed and finally received a pilot's license.

After establishing the Stout Air Services, between Ford Airport in Dearborn and Grand Rapids, Michigan in 1926, one of the first successful scheduled passenger airlines in the United States, he was bought out in 1928 by National Air Transport (NAT), later purchased by United Airlines. NAT did not purchase Stout Air Services because they had such great equipment or routes but because they had developed the detailed business of running a commercial airline. NAT purchased a system.

Stout would go on to develop and produce prototype vehicles such as his *Sky-Car*, a combination car and airplane and his *Scarab*, an extremely innovative automobile for its time. In 1954, Stout obtained the permission of Henry Ford II, to use the original Ford Tri-Motor plans in a venture with the newly formed Hayden Aircraft Company of Bellflower, California, to make a modern version of the Tri-Motor to be called the Stout Bushmaster. While quite similar in dimensions — many of the parts were identical — the market never developed and only two planes were built.

William Benson Mayo (1866 - 1944)

William Mayo started as an office boy with the Boston representative of the Hooven-Owens-Rentschler Company of Hamilton, Ohio, a manufacturer of steam engines. Although lacking a higher formal education, by 1913 he had become a Vice President of the company when he designed and installed nine giant tandem engines using gas and steam to generate power at Ford's new Highland Park plant powerhouse, a feat many experts said wouldn't work.[1] This so impressed Henry Ford that he spent the next several years persuading Mayo to come to work for him as chief plant engineer. For the next several years, Mayo worked for Ford on a part time basis. Finally, in 1916, Mayo agreed to work for Ford full time, but only on his own terms. He obtained the right to retain outside business interests, including connections with his former company. Mayo was the only executive brought into the Ford Motor Company at this level and the only Ford employee ever allowed to retain outside business ties.

Mayo's next major project for Henry Ford was in 1917 when he handled the planning and construction of the mighty Rouge complex in Dearborn, Michigan. Ford continued to rely on Mayo for many and varied projects over the years, including the proposal to build dirigibles for the government in 1919 and negotiating the purchase of the Lincoln Motor Company in 1922. Mayo continued to expand his interest in civic and aviation-related organizations and was a natural choice to oversee Ford's new aviation interests in 1924. By 1929, he was an active member or officer of 17 aviation-related organizations or businesses and a member of at least 20 other civic and local organizations. Mayo also had the title of Chief Engineer when virtually no one had a title in the Ford Motor Company, and during his years as head of the Airplane Division, he was allowed to garner unheard of personal publicity when others were being fired for the same thing. Aero Digest (May 1931), stated that evidence of Henry

Professor Hugo Junkers (left) with William Mayo at Ford Airport in May 1928. A month later, the Fords rejected a Junker proposal for cooperating on technical problems. (HFM 189.5578)

company called the United Aircraft and Transport Company that acquired, among other companies, Pratt & Whitney, Boeing, Hamilton Propeller, Stearman, Northrop, National Air Transport and United Airlines, some of whose board of directors Mayo served on. These connections, with all Mayo's personal publicity and Ford's waning interest in the Aircraft Division, probably fueled Ford's displeasure with Mayo and provided one more reason to sever their relationship. After such an outstanding career with Ford and aviation, his abrupt retirement on September 1, was reported in a very small article in <u>Aero Digest</u> (August 1932), a magazine that had so lavishly praised him just a year earlier. A very typical end to many of Ford's senior executives.

Ford's genius was giving Mayo his opportunity in aviation and ended the tribute to Mayo with: *"if American air transport has a father, that father is named Mayo."*

As early as 1922, Stout, Mayo and Edsel Ford were members of the Aircraft Development Corporation, formed to build the first all-metal dirigible, and Mayo was the single most influential person in Ford's, recognizing Stout's aviation ability and potential.

After Frederick Rentschler, the son of Mayo's previous boss, formed the Pratt & Whitney Aircraft Company to develop the new radial Wasp aircraft engine, Mayo was elected a member of the board of directors and as previously mentioned, Henry Ford later seemed to feel there was a conflict of interest. Rentschler had gone on to form a holding

Harry Joseph Brooks (1902 - 1928)

Harry Brooks was born in 1902, the son of Joseph and Mae Brooks, prosperous farmers in Southfield, Michigan. Like many boys of his generation, Harry was bitten by the aviation bug early as evidenced by his High School year book which listed <u>The Sky Pilot</u> as a book Harry would write. He was the typical All-American boy, participating in football and basketball and being voted the handsomest boy in his class while his girl friend was voted the prettiest girl. On graduating from high school he pursued his aviation interest by becoming a mechanic for a local airstrip owner for $20 a week and flying lessons. In those days, a flying strip was anything from a cow pasture to a mowed hay field with a wind sock. Harry soloed in Lansing, Michigan in 1921[2] and picked up spending money by carrying passengers for local hops around the Detroit area.

Blanche Brooks, Harry's sister, related in a 1996 interview[3] how Henry Ford, partial to fiddler's music, visited the Brooks' farm to listen to an 'Old Time' orchestra whose fiddler was Blanche and Harry's father. A plane Harry was flying happened to be on the front lawn of the Brooks' farm at the time. As Ford had just opened his airport and was in the process of developing his airline, The Ford Air Transport Service, his interest in the mechanically inclined young aviator was natural. Harry probably reminded Henry of his own background — son of farmers, mechanically inclined, unassuming yet self assured and a non-drinker and non-smoker.

Henry took to young Brooks, hiring him August 11, 1925 for 62 1/2 ¢ an hour ($25 a week) working in the airplane plant. For six months, he did everything from riveting the Alclad panels on the big Ford planes to engine maintenance. In February 1926, he was finally taken off the assembly line and appointed a relief pilot for Ford's Air Transport Service at $250 a month. Brooks remained in this position until he acquired the 500 hours of flying time, which was needed to qualify to fly the U.S. Air Mail. Indications of Ford's interest in Harry are contained in an internal memo Schroeder wrote to Mayo on February 6, 1926, regarding Brooks' promotion: *"We have taken extra care with him, knowing the circumstances."* In November of the same year, when Edward Hamilton replaced Major Schroeder as airport manager, Harry was appointed as his assistant and Chief Test Pilot. In his first 21 months as a pilot, he received four increases, raising his pay to $400 a month.

Harry Brooks about 1927. He was Ford's chief test pilot and close friend of Henry Ford. (HFM 0.1685)

Further proof of Ford's fondness for Harry lies in the fact he was allowed to use the single seat *Flivver* airplane as his company car, commuting between his home in Southfield, Michigan and Ford Airport. Considered a careful pilot, he nevertheless attracted attention for such feats as landing on Woodward Avenue in Birmingham, Michigan, to give a talk to a luncheon group and racing Gar Wood's powerboat *Miss America* on the Detroit river. This generated a great deal of local press [4] which described him as Birmingham's Lindbergh. His comparison to Lindbergh was not too far fetched. Both were born in Michigan in 1902 and raised on farms. Both learned to fly in their early years. Both flew the U.S. Air Mail — Lindbergh for the Post Office, from St. Louis to Chicago and Brooks for Ford, from Detroit to Chicago and Cleveland. They knew each other, had flown together and both had set separate long distance flying records. And, they were both extremely fine pilots.

You can readily understand Henry Ford's sense of loss when Harry crashed off the coast of Florida on February 25, 1928.

Notes - Chapter 11

(1) One of these steam-gas power generators, originally installed in the Highland Park plant, is the largest single item on display at the Henry Ford Museum. *(page 145)*

(2) Information on Brooks flying credentials was obtained from his application to fly the U.S. Mail, after being appointed a Ford pilot. *(page 147)*

(3) John Bluth, former editor and publisher of the Detroit Athletic Club's monthly journal, was able to conduct several interviews with Miss Brooks before her death in 1998 and review personal photographs and documents relating to her brother Harry. *(page 147)*

(4) Brooks' publicity was exceeded only by William Mayo, the only other Ford employee allowed to receive such personal press attention. *(page 148)*

12

AVIATION COLLECTION, HENRY FORD MUSEUM

Henry Ford was an avid collector of Americana, especially as it applied to the American way of life from the late 1800s through the early 1900s. This devotion, almost an obsession, resulted in the establishment in October 1929 of the Edison Institute, better known as Henry Ford Museum & Greenfield Village. The Institute was composed of 260 acres which was originally part of the Ford Airport. With his interest in Americana, it was only natural that he acquire airplanes along with stage coaches, automobiles and locomotives as part of his transportation collection.

One of the most significant aviation related items is not an airplane, but a building. It is the Wright brothers' Wright Cycle Co. building from Dayton, Ohio, which was acquired and moved to Greenfield Village in 1936. It was in this shop that the first airplane capable of controlled flight was built and then flown at Kitty Hawk, North Carolina in 1903 by Wilbur and Orville Wright.

In 1961, a panel of aviation experts selected the twelve most significant aircraft of all time.[1] Of the nine piston-driven planes on the list, the Henry Ford Museum has eight planes that are representative of the ones selected. The only missing example of the piston-powered planes is the Wright's Flyer, the first plane to fly.[2] The eight planes are indicated by a star (*) in front of the listing. All aircraft are listed by date of manufacture.

* 1909 BLERIOT XI. This monoplane is similar to the one flown by Louis Bleriot in the first crossing of the English Channel in 1909. In a 1928 letter, Bleriot-Aeronautique, the manufacturer, states that this plane was number 169, built December 7, 1909 and referred to as their Cross Channel type. Purchased by Henry Ford in 1928.

Engine:	3 cyl, 25 hp, Anzani
Length:	25' 8"
Wingspan:	28' 8"

1915 LAIRD. Emile Laird was one of the early exhibition pilots and used this bi-plane in one of the first aerial loop-the-loops, quite a daring stunt for the times. In 1917, Katherine Stinson, a famous aviatrix and sister of the famous pilot and airplane manufacturer Eddie Stinson, took this plane on an exhibition tour of China and Japan. Donated to the museum in 1936 by Emile Laird.

Engine:	6 cyl, 45 hp, Anzani
Speed:	65-70 mph, maximum
Length:	19' 5"
Wingspan:	25' 4"

* 1916 CURTISS MODEL F Flying Boat.
This bi-plane is similar to the one Glenn Curtiss developed in 1911 as the first successful flying boat. It was purchased by Henry Ford for Evangeline Dahlinger who was in effect his administrative assistant for personal affairs and the first woman pilot licensed in Michigan. She was the wife of Ray Dahlinger, manager of Ford's farms and the man who "fixed things" for Mr. Ford. Donated to the museum by Ray Dahlinger.

Engine:	8 cyl, 150 hp, Hispano-Suiza
Speed:	69 mph, maximum
Length:	28' 10"
Wingspan:	49' 10"

1916 STANDARD J-1. This type of bi-plane was used by the Army Air Service for primary training 1916 - 1918. Equipped with an unreliable 125 hp Hall-Scott engine, they were phased out by the Army in favor of the Curtiss JN-4-D and many Standards remained in their original shipping crates until after the war. Following the war, they were inexpensive and proved to be a popular barnstorming plane when fitted with a Curtiss OX-5 or Hispano-Suiza engine. Donated to the museum in 1938 by Ernest Hall.

Engine:	8 cyl, 180 hp Hispano-Suiza
Speed:	102 mph, maximum
Length:	28'
Wingspan:	45'

1917 CURTISS JN 4-D, *Canuck.* This is the Canadian version of the famous Curtiss

Jenny bi-plane that was the primary U.S. pilot training airplane during and after World War I. There were nearly 11,000 of the U.S. and Canadian versions of this plane built, creating a great surplus following the armistice in November 1918. Most were sold in the United States for about $100 used and $600 new, and resulted in nearly every pilot, or would-be pilot, using them to barnstorm the country for many years, delighting a public recently awakened to the marvels of the air. It was finally grounded in 1928 by the new licensing requirements issued by the Department of Commerce. Donated to the museum by Ray Dahlinger.

Engine:	8 cyl, 90 hp, Curtiss OX-5
Speed:	79 mph, maximum
Length:	27' 4"
Wingspan:	43' 7"

* 1920 DAYTON-WRIGHT RB-1 Racer.
This high-wing monoplane was designed by Howard Rhinehart and Milton Baumann, thus the RB designation. It was the first aircraft to utilize a retractable landing gear and a variable wing camber developed by Charles Grant and used on many of today's jet aircraft. Built by the Dayton-Wright Airplane Company, whose chief consulting engineer was Orville Wright, the company was organized by, among others, Charles Kettering, a prominent researcher and inventor who eventually became president of General Motors. It was specifically designed to participate in the Gorden Bennett Air Race of 1920. Unfortunately, it was forced out after the first

lap due to a broken cable. Donated to the museum in 1940 by the University of Michigan.

Engine:	6 cyl, 250 hp, Hall-Scott
Speed:	200 mph, maximum
Length:	22' 8"
Wingspan:	21' 2"

1925 FOKKER F VIIa-3m. This high-wing monoplane was the first of the highly successful single engine Fokker F VIIa models modified by adding an additional engine under each wing. It was purchased by Lt. Comdr. Richard Byrd for his famous flight over the North Pole in 1926 and named the *Josephine Ford* in honor of Edsel Ford's daughter. The plane, made of a fabric covered steel frame and plywood wings, was a great success, becoming one of the outstanding transport planes of the times, until the all-metal Ford Tri-Motor was introduced. This plane was purchased by Edsel Ford after Byrd's Arctic trip in 1926. (see chapter 7)

Engine:	Three 9 cyl, 200 hp, Wright Whirlwind
Speed:	118 mph, maximum
Length:	47' 10"
Wingspan:	63' 4"

1926 FORD *FLIVVER*. This is a single seat low-wing monoplane and represented Ford's first attempt to build a *Flivver* of the air. A slightly larger Ford *Flivver* built in 1927 broke the small plane distance record in 1928. (see chapter 10)

Engine:	3 cyl, 35 hp, Anzani
Speed:	85 mph, maximum
Length:	16'
Wingspan:	21' 9"

1927 BOEING 40-B2. This bi-plane was one of a fleet of 24 planes built by Boeing Aircraft Company for their subsidiary Boeing Air Transport (later United Air Lines), for the first scheduled transcontinental mail and passenger service between San Francisco and Chicago. The pilot was located in an open cockpit behind an enclosed, two passenger compartment and nearly 1,000 pounds of mail. It was donated to the museum in 1940 by United Air Lines.

Engine:	9 cyl, 500 hp, Pratt & Whitney Hornet
Speed:	120 mph, maximum
Length:	33' 4"
Wingspan:	44' 2"

* 1927 RYAN BROUGHAM NYP. This high-wing monoplane is an original Ryan monoplane patterned on the *Spirit of St. Louis* and built shortly after Lindbergh's successful crossing of the Atlantic Ocean in 1927. It was refurbished to the original *Spirit of St. Louis* specifications and used in the movie *The Spirit of St. Louis,* starring James Stewart in 1957. Charles Lindbergh inspected the plane after it was rebuilt and, according to Mr. Stewart: *"he approved everything we had done"* to duplicate his plane. Donated to the museum by James Stewart in 1957. (see chapter 9)

Engine: 9 cyl, 220 hp, Wright
           Whirlwind J-5
Speed: 112 mph, cruising
Length: 27' 8"
Wingspan: 46'

1927 STINSON, SM-1 DETROITER. This high-wing monoplane was purchased by Edward Schlee, President of Wayco Oil Company in Detroit, Michigan, named the *Miss Wayco* and entered in the 1927 National Air Tour with its builder, Eddie Stinson as pilot. The first place finish so impressed Schlee that he renamed the ship *Pride of Detroit* and, with his pilot, William Brock, attempted an around-the-world flight in October 1927, just five months after Lindbergh had completed his epic flight across the Atlantic. Traveling eastward from Detroit they reached Tokyo, Japan where they heeded the pleas of family and friends and declined to attempt the final leg of the flight across the Pacific. Everything considered, it was still an outstanding performance. This plane was one of the most famous light aircraft produced from the mid 1920s to the mid 1930s. It was purchased by the museum in 1932.

Engine: 9 cyl, 200 hp, Wright
           Whirlwind J-5
Speed: 113 mph, cruising
Length: 32' 8"
Wingspan: 46' 8"

1928 FORD 4AT-B. This high-wing monoplane was used by Richard Byrd in his historic trip over the South Pole in 1929. There were numerous modifications to the standard 4AT-B, primarily to increase power and fuel capacity and to reduce weight. It was named the *Floyd Bennett* after Byrd's North Pole pilot who had died while participating in the rescue of the *Bremen* flyers. It was placed in the Ford museum after being recovered from the South Pole in 1935. (see chapter 7)

Engine: Two 9 cyl, 220 hp, Wright
           Whirlwind, One 9 cyl,
           520 hp, Wright Cyclone
Speed: 128 mph, maximum with
           three Whirlwinds
Length: 45' 8"
Wingspan: 74'

* 1928 JUNKERS W-33. This low-wing monoplane is covered in corrugated Alclad as is the Ford Tri-Motor. Named the *Bremen* after the luxury transatlantic ocean liner of the North German Lloyd's line, this plane was used in the first east - west crossing of the Atlantic in April 1928. It was a more demanding flight than Lindbergh's the previous year as they had to fight the headwinds which, as tailwinds, had benefited Lindbergh. The *Bremen* was donated to the Museum of the City of New York by Baron von Huenefeld, a major backer and one of the three participants in the historic flight, on behalf of all the backers, most of whom were from Bremen, Germany. The plane was shipped back to Germany for restoration and returned to New York in May 1929, where it was displayed in Grand Central Station to a first day crowd of 15,000 people. Lacking space, The New York museum placed the plane on loan to the Smithsonian Institute, Washington, D.C. in 1930. In 1936, the Smithsonian advised that it was returning the *Bremen* to New York and at that time the decision was made by the New York museum to donate it to the Edison Institute. In April 1997, the *Bremen* was placed on a six year loan and returned to the city of Bremen, Germany to celebrate the 70th anniversary of its historic flight across the Atlantic.

Engine: 6 cyl, 310 hp, Junkers L-5
Speed: 97 mph, cruising
Length: 34' 6"
Wingspan: 58' 3"

1929 LOCKHEED VEGA 5B. A high-wing monoplane, this type of plane holds more overland and overseas records than any other type plane, with one being flown by Wiley Post in his around-the-world solo flight in 1933. This plane was initially used as a demonstrator by Lockheed and its log book includes such names as Charles Lindbergh and Amelia Earhart. It was also used by Rear Admiral Donald McMillan in 1931 for one of his many Arctic trips for a survey expedition of Labrador and Greenland, mapping 50,000 square miles of additional terrain. Purchased by the museum in 1968.

Engine: 9 cyl, 300 hp, Pratt &
Whitney Wasp, Jr.
Speed: 160 mph, maximum
Length: 27' 6"
Wingspan: 41'

1931 PITCAIRN PCA-2. Although the basic design of the Autogyro was by Juan de la Cierva of Spain, this aircraft contains many innovations designed by Pitcairn engineers. Many of Pitcairn's Autogyro patents were crucial to the development of the helicopter during World War II. This was the first American Autogyro built for commercial use and was delivered to the Detroit News in February 1931. A major problem was encountered in licensing the craft as the Department of Commerce had no precedents on which to base its approval. Donated to the museum in 1934 by William Scripps, President of the Detroit News.

Engine: 300 hp Wright Whirwind
Speed: 123 mph, maximum
Wingspan: 20' 1"
Rotor: 45' 10" diameter

* 1939 DOUGLAS DC-3. This low-wing monoplane logged 84,875 flying hours, more than any other single commercial aircraft in history. Replacing the Ford Tri-Motor as the aircraft of choice for passenger airlines, more than 10,000 were built. It formed the backbone of military air transportation in World War II under the designation C-47 and was affectionately called the *Gooney Bird*. It was retired from service and donated to the museum in 1975 by North Central Airlines and was the last plane to land at Ford Airport.

Engine: Two 9 cyl, 1000 hp,
Wright Cyclone
Speed: 180 mph, cruising
Length: 64' 6"
Wingspan: 95'

* 1939 VOUGHT-SIKORSKY VS 300A.
This was the first practical helicopter in the United States and, using a 90 hp Franklin engine, established a world endurance record in 1941 by remaining in the air for one hour and 33 minutes. This helicopter had a range of 75 miles and could carry a 250 pound load to an altitude of 4,000 feet. It was donated to the museum in 1943 by its designer Igor Sikorsky.

Engine:	4 cyl, 75 hp, Lycoming O-134-C
Speed:	70 mph, maximum
Length:	27' 11"
Rotor	30' 2" diameter

* 1946 PIPER CUB J-3. This high-wing monoplane was the Model T of the air, with over 30,000 built between 1931 and 1947 with virtually no engineering changes. The plane sold for under $1,000 in 1941. More U.S. pilots learned to fly in this type of airplane than any other. Donated to the museum by the Piper Aircraft Corporation in 1961.

Engine:	4 cyl, 65 hp, Continental A65-8
Speed:	87 mph, maximum
Length:	28' 8"
Wingspan:	34' 7"

Notes - Chapter 12

(1) In 1961, <u>Popular Science</u> magazine selected four aviation experts to select the 12 most significant aircraft. The panel consisted of: Jimmy Doolittle who built his first do-it-yourself airplane in 1910. He went on to become a civilian racing pilot and Army General, commanding the 8th Air Forces in Europe during World War II. Dr. Jerome Hunsaker, designer of the airship *Shenandoah* and the NC-4 flying boats, which were the first to cross the Atlantic ocean in 1919. He was also an aeronautical-engineering professor and a member of the National Advisory Committee on Aeronautics for 15 years. Grover Loening, aircraft inventor, designer and builder and the first engineer employed by the Wright brothers. Dr. John Victory, the first employee of the National Advisory Committee on Aeronautics (NACA) when it was founded in 1915 and serving there until his retirement in 1960. *(page 149)*

(2) At the same time that Ford was negotiating with the Wrights for their building, he was also trying to obtain the Wright brothers' first airplane. It had been sent to London for display due to a dispute with the Smithsonian Institute in Washington, DC over who made the first controlled flight. The dispute was finally resolved in the Wright brothers' favor and the plane returned to the United States in 1948. *(page 149)*

13

THE END OF COMMERCIAL AVIATION

The End Of Pre-War Aviation Activities

The roaring twenties was a time of unbridled optimism for the future, and aviation certainly was on the leading edge. The stock market was booming and new aviation issues were snatched up as fast as they appeared. The stock of Seaboard Air Line skyrocketed, driven up by speculators that didn't know it was an east coast railroad. Wright Aeronautical, an aircraft engine builder, whose stock sold for $20 from 1922 to 1925, reached $300 in 1929. To justify this enormous investment in aviation during 1929, manufacturers should have sold about 25,000 aircraft annually but actually sold 5,500. In the face of this booming economy, however, the sales of Henry Ford's beloved Model T were declining. Because of his refusal to modernize his vehicles and compete head to head with other manufacturers, especially General Motors, Ford lost sales leadership to Chevrolet. The mighty Rouge Plant shut down in late 1927 to re-tool for the new Ford Model A. With production curtailed, Ford lost[1] $42,000,000 in 1927 and another $72,000,000 in 1928. Ford's car sales, however, rebounded in 1929 reaching a near record and his airplane sales were also improving.

The euphoria of the roaring twenties came to a screeching halt with the crash of the stock market in October 1929. The value of 46 aircraft company stocks plunged 56% between May 24 and November 29, 1929 and commercial airplane sales dropped 80%. Ford's automobile and truck production plummeted from a near record 1,870,257 vehicles in 1929 to a 17 year low of 395,956 in 1932. Ford profits also plunged to a loss of $54,000,000 in 1931 and another $44,000,000 loss in 1932. Unemployment skyrocketed from 3.2% in 1929 to 23.6% in 1932 while the average annual wage for those still working sank from $1,356 to $754.

The irony of these depressing figures is that the number of airline passengers carried increased dramatically — from 6,000 in 1925 to 165,000 in 1929 to over 450,000 in 1931. The increase in passenger traffic was primarily due to the greater number of routes generated by the new Air Mail contracts and the fact that airline expenses were being substantially subsidized by the Post Office Department. However, even with the subsidies and the increase in passengers, it resulted in few

Mooring mast being pulled over by cables attached to several trucks. It was the end of an era for Ford and the end of the landmark in Dearborn, Michigan. (HFM B.111064)

additional orders for new aircraft. Civilian airplane production fell from a record 5,516 airplanes in 1929 to 1,988 in 1931.

Peak monthly production of 25 Ford planes was achieved in June 1929 and Ford would produce only 34 planes in the next two and a half years. A Ford memo in July 1932 forecast a bleak future: *"Outlook for the next five years: We can build, in about six months, all the planes the commercial trade requires for the next four years."* Airplane manufacturing at Ford was practically shut down by August 1932. An August inventory listed two planes in Ford's Air Transport Service, nine used planes on hand, two new planes available for sale, and two planes 75% completed, awaiting a buyer for finishing touches. While the giant 32 passenger 14AT was listed as "in process", it is doubtful if any further work was being done. The last two new Tri-Motors, delivered to Pan American Airways, were finished in May 1933, almost a year later and the last of the used planes was sold in September 1934. Selling prices, which ranged up to $50,000 for the 4AT, had

With the bloom off the airplane manufacturing business and the Depression causing a disaster in the automotive industry, even Henry Ford with his immense wealth, had to concentrate on his core business.

Though he would no longer be part of it, Henry Ford's efforts to promote the safety

Henry and Clara Ford watching the mast being toppled, October 16, 1946. This was one of Henry Ford's last public appearances as he died April 7, 1947. (FMC 833.83419.1)

dropped to $40,000 and the 5AT model had dropped from $60,000 to $50,000, with Ford's and the engine manufacturers warranty covering parts for 90 days. In April 1940, seven years after the last new Ford tri-Motor was sold, prices had plummeted to $3,500 for a renovated Ford 4AT.[2]

and reliability of commercial aviation was paying off. Ford's departure from aviation gave Boeing and Douglas the incentive and opportunity to design and produce modern aircraft that some say they were reluctant to do as long as Ford retained the potential to dominate commercial aviation. The introduc-

Mooring mast on ground awaiting the scavenger's torch. (FMC 833.83419.10)

tion of the Boeing 247, announced in May 1932, and the Douglas DC-2s and DC-3s a short time later, made Ford's old *Tin Goose* a tough sell to airlines in America, although they continued in service in many Latin American countries for the next thirty years. The last Tri-Motor was trimmed up and sold June 8, 1933, the airplane factory closed down and the few remaining men were laid off. A small repair staff was retained to service existing planes until December 1936 when all remaining men qualified in needed automotive skills were transferred to the Rouge plant, returning as needed to fabricate service parts for Tri-Motor owners. Small parts continued to be supplied to Tri-Motor owners into the mid 1940s.

The last pre-war aviation happening at Ford Airport was the October 23, 1934 stratospheric balloon ascent of Dr. Jean Piccard and his wife Jeannette for the purpose of studying the origins and nature of Cosmic Rays. The balloon was piloted by Mrs.

Piccard, the first and only woman in the United States at that time licensed as a balloon pilot and the first time any woman had piloted a balloon on a stratospheric flight. By reaching 57,979 feet, she not only set a woman's altitude record but also became the first woman to enter the stratosphere. In addition to making the Ford Airport available for the ascent, William Gassett, a Ford radio engineer, developed a small VHF radio to provide ground to air communication for the flight. The decision to provide a radio proved providential as the sky was so heavily overcast for the 5 hour 225 mile trip, which ended in Cadiz, Ohio, that at one point the Piccards thought they were over the Atlantic ocean. While weight restrictions limited the weight of the radio package to ten pounds, it performed superbly, keeping a chase car in contact with the balloon to the point of descent where they witnessed the touchdown.

The Ford airport continued to function on a limited basis although a test track was laid out around the runways in 1938. Prior to this, Ford cars had been tested on the public roadways around the Dearborn area. In 1938, while the Airport was officially open, the Civil Aviation Authority <u>Weekly Notice to Airmen</u> (August 23, 1938) advised: *"Airmen should circle Ford Airport twice before landing on field."* Ford had requested this so automobiles being tested could pull out of their way. World War II rejuvenated Ford Airport and it was actively used by the military and later civil aircraft until June 1947.

The dirigible mooring mast, which had been a Dearborn landmark and had identified the Ford Airport for so long, was toppled October 26, 1946 and the terminal building was demolished on August 11, 1961. A propeller repair and overhaul department which had been maintained at the airport until mid 1948 was sold to Commercial Aircraft Inc. of Willow Run, Michigan. It had been the only completely equipped propeller facility in the Midwest and this sale severed the last link between Ford Airport and aviation.

Today, Ford Airport is the home of Ford's Dearborn Proving Grounds. The airplane factory, with a new facade, is devoted to Experimental Vehicles, while the hangar building, housing Ford's Experimental Engine group, is still in its original form and visible

The Ford Air Transportation Office was organized in 1941 to hire pilots to test the B-24 bombers being built at Ford's Willow Run plant. Reading left to right: Hal Henning, Ford's Chief Pilot, Charles Sorensen, Ford's Production boss, Benson Ford, Edsel Ford's son, and Edsel Ford. (Hudek 833.76795A)

from Oakwood Boulevard. These two buildings and the world's first concrete runway are all that remain of Henry Ford's Airport. The Dearborn Inn is listed on the National Register of Historic Places and the Ford Airport has been designated as a Michigan Historical Site.

The New Ford Air Transportation Office

The successor to the Ford Air Transportation Service (ATS), which terminated in 1932, was the Ford Air Transportation Office (ATO) formed November 11, 1941 in the hangar at Ford Airport in Dearborn, Michigan. Manager and chief test pilot Hal Henning was hired along with seven pilots, including Charles Lindbergh, to form the secret Test Flight Department in connection with the Ford B-24 bomber plant at Willow Run, Michigan.

Following the war, the Air Transportation Office was expanded to provide private transportation for Ford executives and operations continued at Ford Airport in Dearborn.[3] In 1947, the Ford Motor Company, losing large sums of money, was in no position to upgrade their airport facilities. Fortunately, Wayne County Airport in Romulus, Michigan, now known as Detroit Metro, had been developed by the Army during the war into a modern airport with an up-to-date radio range finder and modern traffic control facilities. Ford moved their operations to an existing hangar at the Wayne County Airport and Ford Airport in Dearborn was closed for good.[4]

On May 28, 1975, Ford airport was opened one last time for the arrival of a 1939 Douglas DC-3 airplane. The DC-3 had been donated to the Henry Ford Museum by North Central Airlines, who would merge with Republic Airlines, who in turn would be absorbed by Northwest Airlines.

Notes - Chapter 13

(1)   Although privately owned, Ford was required by law to file an annual balance sheet with the State of Massachusetts. By comparing year-to-year balance sheet statements, Ford's estimated profit or loss for a given year could be determined. Ford's losses in 1927 and 1928 of $114 million equates to $1.1 billion in current dollars while the losses in 1931 and 1932 of $98 million equals $1.2 billion in today's dollars. *(page 155)*

(2)   By 1988 the few remaining flying Fords were commanding substantial premiums. 5AT-8, restored to original condition by Harrah's Automotive Museum in Reno, Nevada, was sold for $1,500,000. *(page 157)*

(3)   The first Ford Company plane, obtained in December 1941, for pilot training and transportation, was a Grumman G-21 Goose amphibian. Following the war, Ford ATO operated a Beech C-45 and two C-47s (DC-3) purchased from the Air Force. From this small beginning, Ford ATO has operated 35 aircraft of 17 different types over the years, the largest being a Boeing 727 jetliner from 1972 to 1974. *(page 160)*

(4)   In November 1963, Ford ATO relocated to a new 72,000 square foot hangar at Detroit Metro and currently operates from that location. In addition, Ford operates an Air Transportation Department in England. With the consolidation of all Ford European activities under Ford of Europe, there developed an enormous increase in personnel traveling between Ford's various marketing and manufacturing sites in Europe. The Ford Air Transportation Department was inaugurated at Stansted Airfield, outside of London on August 14, 1967, utilizing a hangar built by the U.S. Army Air Force in World War II. In 1989, Ford moved into a new hangar complex at Stansted and the old hangar was removed and re-erected at the Imperial War Museum Airfield at Duxford, Cambridgeshire. *(page 160)*

14

AVIATION WAR PRODUCTION

World War I

The war in Europe was expanding at an alarming rate in 1915, adding nation after nation to the list of belligerents and hundreds of thousands of soldiers to the mounting casualty rolls. Henry Ford was an outspoken pacifist who had often expressed his view that war only profited politicians and greedy businessmen. By late 1915, Henry Ford had been approached by a pacifist group, who viewed him as one of their own and persuaded him that he had the power to bring peace to Europe by making a direct personal appeal to the leaders of the warring nations. Ford, feeling he might be able to influence these leaders, chartered the Scandinavian-American ocean liner *Oscar II*. On December 4, 1915, he set sail to Norway with a boatload of supporters and newsmen. For months, they had been proclaiming their mission was world peace and that they would: *"get the boys out of the trenches by Christmas."*

While it was undoubtedly an earnest effort on Henry Ford's part to bring peace, it was doomed to failure, and it was subject to unrelenting ridicule by the world's press. But,

while the press scorned his efforts, it generated an enormous amount of good will towards Henry Ford by the common folks. At least he had tried and as one song that was published about his trip proclaimed: *Mr. Ford You've Got The Right Idea!*

During this period, America, while watching the devastation taking place in Europe, saw no reason to become involved and, with the Atlantic Ocean as a buffer, took no action to increase its armed forces until the Germans resorted to unrestricted submarine warfare, sinking a number of United States merchant vessels. On April 6, 1917, the United States finally declared war on Germany.

Starting with the Aviation Section of the U.S. Army's Signal Corps, equipped with only a few obsolete airplanes, a massive effort was immediately put forth to design and build all sorts of war machinery, virtually none of which would reach the front lines in Europe. The war ended 19 months later with the United States' only significant, though most vital, contribution being its manpower.

Aircraft Engines

While the government bureaucrats were trying to sort out just what sort of war materials were needed and what the United States should produce, Henry Ford was trying to obtain a captured German airplane with a Mercedes engine. In September 1917, Ford exchanged wires with Percival Perry, Man-

One of the major American war products decided on was the American designed *Liberty* aircraft engine that Michigan automakers were requested to build. As a result, Ford's aviation contribution to the war effort was the production of this engine designed by Elbert Hall of Hall-Scott Motor Car Company and Jesse Vincent of Packard Motor Car Company. Designed in 1917 to be an 8 or 12 cylinder engine, it was felt that an 8 cylinder, 225 hp version of the Liberty engine would provide the power necessary for aerial warfare in 1918 with the 12 cylinder, 400 hp engine scheduled for production in 1919. Aviation was developing so fast that only 90 days later, the need for more powerful engines was recognized and all efforts were directed to producing only the 12 cylinder version of the engine. In addition to producing the engine, Ford

The Liberty aircraft engine was the main aviation item produced by Ford Motor Company in World War I. (HFM 833.23062)

ager of the Ford works in England, exhorting him to obtain from the British government one of the captured German planes. Ford's intent was to examine the engine and then design and build an airplane motor for the United States. Perry advised Ford that while such a plane and engine was available, the British government would not act without a request from the United States government and so nothing happened. The bureaucracy prevailed.[1]

solved a most serious problem in the Liberty engine by developing a special process for making the bearings in the crankcase and connecting rods that were causing repeated engine failures. Ford also devised an inexpensive method for cylinder construction. The cylinders were originally bored out of solid steel forgings, a laborious and expensive operation. Ford engineers produced a cylinder from steel tubing that reduced the labor and material costs from $19.75 each to

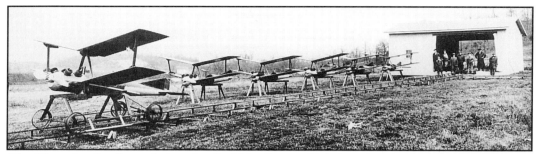

The "Kettering Bug" was designed to fly 200 miles at which time the wings would fall off and it would crash on the target. Ford designed and built the engine. Developed too late to be used in World War I. (HFM 189.63700)

$8.25. (This ability to reduce costs through manufacturing innovations would be Ford's trademark for all war production efforts through World War II.) Ford built all 433,826 of the new cylinders produced and 3,950 of the total 20,478 Liberty engines produced.

Another little known World War I aviation contribution was Ford's development of an engine for a buzz bomb, a secret program that only became known years later. Captain Hap Arnold (commanding General of the Army Air Forces in World War II) directed a program to develop a low cost, long range, self-guided, self-propelled torpedo called a robot bomb, later known as the *Kettering Bug*. The missile was to be accurate up to 200 miles, carry a 200 pound war head and cost no more than $200. Charles Kettering, the renowned General Motors inventor, was in charge of the project and Ford was charged with developing the engine. C. H. Wills, a Ford engineer in charge of Ford's Liberty engine project and one of the chief designers of the Ford Model T, was given the task of developing the new engine. It was a hori-

zontal, two cylinder, air-cooled, 40 hp engine weighing 151 pounds that could be mass produced for $40. It was mounted on a 12 foot bi-plane with a 14 foot wing span and designed and built to fly 4 or 5 hours — just long enough to reach its objective. Flight direction was determined by gyroscopic controls and distance was controlled by a cam, set for a predetermined number of engine revolutions needed to reach the target. When the engine had turned the prescribed number of revolutions, the cam would withdraw the bolts holding on the wings and the fuselage would drop to the ground like a bomb. Final testing didn't take place until October 1919, nearly a year after the armistice and the project was not pursued further until the beginning of World War II. At that time, it was decided that major targets in Germany were too far from British bases for a Bug type bomb to be effective.[2]

One other World War I defense project, while not aviation related, did hint at the future. It was Ford's decision to build submarine chasers, called *Eagle Patrol Boats* for the Navy.

The government subsidized the building of the first Ford factory at the Rouge to turn out these 200 foot, 615 ton steel boats on an assembly line basis. Nobody had ever produced boats of this size in such a manner. On January 18, 1918, the Navy authorized Ford to proceed with building these boats and in ten months a building was erected, tools obtained and set up, men trained and twelve boats actually launched. People shouldn't have been surprised when Ford again used the assembly line techniques to build airplanes in 1926 and then again in 1941.

World War II

When Ford's Greenfield Village was closed by the war in early 1942, Charles LaCroix, Assistant Director of the village, was given the assignment by Henry Ford to write Ford's history of the war. Ford told him to: *"write me something I'll enjoy reading, not just a lot of statistics."* In completing his assignment, LaCroix produced eight summary volumes, backed up by fifty supplementary volumes covering in great detail the many facets of Ford's war production. Much of Ford's World War II experience detailed here was drawn from LaCroix's extensive documentation.

Very much like World War I, the United States was not militarily ready to enter World War II, in spite of President Roosevelt's best efforts to re-arm the nation and support Great Britain in their struggle against Nazi Germany. But unlike 1917, we had at least started taking steps to produce war materials for Great Britian and France, and many government contracts had been let by 1940 and early 1941. Ford, an outspoken critic of 'Roosevelt's war', had along with all other auto manufacturers, accepted a number of war production contracts prior to the Japanese attack on Pearl Harbor on December 7, 1941. By now, Henry Ford was committed to building for American defense.

Henry Ford was in his late 70s, and as is now known, was not always totally aware or in command of what was happening in his company. In fairness, though, he had established and developed the organization that was able to contribute so mightily to the nation's war production. He approved of the company's war efforts, participated in major policy decisions and spent a great deal of time at the Willow Run bomber plant. That said, however, there were tremendous problems with the in-fighting between Harry Bennett, Ford's fixer and Charles Sorensen, Ford's production manager which worsened with the death of Edsel Ford in May 1943.

While Ford was not the largest producer of war materials during World War II, it got the lion's share of publicity, due primarily to the extraordinary, many said unbelievable, forecast of building one of the large B-24 bombers an hour and the sheer magnitude of the new bomber factory at Willow Run, Michigan. Production of a giant airplane on an assembly line had never been done before and the enormity of building these large airplanes, in the numbers forecast, grabbed the public's imagination. Throughout the war, a story on Willow Run was always good for newspaper articles and magazine features although much of it was negative in the first year or so. Unlike other producers, Ford did very little advertising regarding its production of airplanes, tanks and jeeps. He felt, and rightly so, with all the free press he was receiving, people knew what Ford was doing. With all this free press, it is not surprising that a Roper survey in the spring of 1945 found that only

Henry Kaiser and his shipyards ranked higher than Henry Ford in people's opinion of which businessman did the most to aid the war effort.

Aircraft

In January 1941, Edsel Ford and Charles Sorensen, at the request of the U.S. Government, visited Consolidated Aircraft in California to examine the possibility of building aircraft wings for Consolidated's B-24 bomber. Sorensen relates in his autobiography, <u>My Forty Years With Ford</u>, as he

The massive Willow Run bomber plant and airport in Washtenaw County, Michigan. Enough concrete was used in the runways to build a two lane highway 22 miles long. (Hudek 833.82126.5A)

Ford's twin assembly line for B-24 bombers. A sharp right turn was made at end of assembly lines to insure the plant would not extend into Wayne County which would probably result in higher taxes after the war. (Hudek 833.80626.7)

watched the piecemeal construction of the massive B-24 bomber at the Consolidated factory, he realized it was much like the way Ford had built Model N automobiles 35 years earlier. Sorensen was sure the wing assemblies made by Ford would never fit the fuselages built by Consolidated. Their planes were literally hand built and it would be nearly impossible to mate them to the precision manufactured wings Ford would build. Backed by Edsel Ford, Sorensen stated: *"We'll make the complete plane or nothing at all,"* and countered with a plan to build the entire bomber based on the precision automotive assembly line methods Ford had pioneered. Ford claimed to an incredulous press: *they could build 540 bombers a month versus Consolidated's very ambitious goal of 350 a year.* Sorensen's proposal was accepted and Ford's problems started.

Consolidated, while welcoming Ford's participation as a sub-contractor, was wary, as were the other major airplane manufacturers, about Ford's entrance into the aviation field and its implication for postwar competition. They were not happy that Ford was to build the whole plane but, in the spirit of cooperation, they took the attitude that they would teach Ford how to build airplanes. Ford men, on the other hand, having seen how Consolidated built planes by hand, took the attitude that they were going to show the aviation industry how to build planes better and faster. The first Ford hurdle was in getting a set of plans from Consolidated. Up to date, detailed plans did not exist as Consolidated had made running changes that were never recorded. Ford had to send their own engineers and draftsmen to Consolidated to make a set of complete, up-to-date plans.

Ford-Built Consolidated Liberator Bomber

Watch The Fords Go By!

FLEETS of mighty bombers are coming from Willow Run! Fleets of giant four-engined *Fords* with wings and heavily armored bodies able to carry tons of bombs to the Axis!

These Ford-built Consolidated Liberator bombers are not only in production . . . *they're in volume production!* And they're leaving Willow Run in a steady stream for service throughout the world.

Never before Willow Run has anything so big and complex as this Liberator bomber been built on an interchangeable mass-production basis. Some said it couldn't be done . . . that frequent design changes would make mass production *impossible*. But army men knew that failure to produce aircraft in mass would prove disastrous. They knew that Victory demanded what seemed *impossible*—and they relied on Ford to do it.

The army was right. What many thought *impossible has been done* at Willow Run!

There were difficulties such as manpower shortages, the training of inexperienced workers and the curtailment of transportation.

But today Willow Run is doing what Ford promised! The plant is producing bombers in volume . . . *and on schedule!*

At other Ford plants across the nation, fleets of *war models* are being delivered every day. These include M-4 tanks, M-10 tank destroyers, Ford-built 2000-hp Pratt & Whitney engines for which Ford has received the Army-Navy "E", and many other Victory models listed below.

As you *watch these Fords go by* on their way to your sons and brothers at the front, remember that their quantity and quality reflect the feeling of the whole Ford organization that . . . *no effort short of Victory is enough.*

Ford Mass-Production Lines Deliver Fleets of Weapons

M-4 TANKS . . . M-10 TANK DESTROYERS . . . GUN MOUNTS
PRATT & WHITNEY AIRCRAFT ENGINES . . . AMPHIBIAN JEEPS
CONSOLIDATED LIBERATOR BOMBERS . . . TANK ENGINES
UNIVERSAL CARRIERS . . . TRANSPORT GLIDERS . . . JEEPS
ARMY TRUCKS . . . ARMOR PLATE . . . AIRCRAFT GENERATORS
TRUCK AND JEEP ENGINES . . . RATE-OF-CLIMB INDICATORS
TURBO-SUPERCHARGERS . . . MAGNESIUM CASTINGS

This list does not include other important Victory models now in production that cannot be named due to wartime conditions.

LISTEN TO "WATCH THE WORLD GO BY" FEATURING EARL GODWIN, EVERY NIGHT 8:00 P. M. E. W. T. ON THE BLUE NETWORK

★ ★ Buy U. S. War Bonds And Stamps ★ ★

F O R D M O T O R C O M P A N Y

F U L L P R O D U C T I O N F O R V I C T O R Y

"Watch The Fords Go By!", one of the few ads run by Ford during World War II. The slogan was first used in 1908 to advertise the first Ford Model T automobile.

Ground clearing was started in March 1941, at Willow Run, Michigan,[3] on what was to be the largest factory in the world with 2,500,000 square feet of floor space and an assembly line nearly a mile long. One year later, Time magazine (March 23, 1942) would call it: *"the most enormous room in the history of man."* Like most other Ford buildings, it was designed by Albert Kahn. It was built in an "L" shape to prevent the final assembly line running across the Washtenaw County line into Wayne County (Detroit) and the potential of higher taxes when converted to civilian production after the war. Six 160 foot wide runways were built, the longest being 7,365 feet. Enough concrete was used in their construction to make a two lane highway 22 miles long. Three hangars were built, each with a 45 ton door that slid up and down with the touch of an electric button, with the largest capable of housing twenty B-24s at one time. In all, there was almost 5,000,000 square feet of roofed buildings erected on the 1,878 acres devoted to the project. While the building was finished in November 1941, it took ten more months for the first B-24 to be produced.

Ford Motor Company in conjunction with the Army Air Force sent B-24 displays to various cities to stimulate war bond sales. The author, in school at the time, visited this display when set up on the grounds of the Washington Monument in October 1943. (Gary Bassett 833.7879.1)

In the interim, while crews of workmen were working in relays to complete the facility for the B-24, jigs and dies were installed in the old airplane factory at Ford Airport in Dearborn, Michigan. This provided the opportunity to not only train new employees in new ways of working, but also enabled Ford to solve many assembly problems prior to full scale production. A further benefit was they began producing bomber sub-assemblies for knock-down kits to be shipped to Consolidated for final assembly.

 Most people couldn't understand why it was taking so long for Ford to get going. They just could not comprehend the enormity of starting up a plant this size to build an item with 152,235 parts held together by over 360,000 rivets. However, when you consider the enormous amount of scarce specialized machinery and fixtures that had to be de-signed and fabricated to build planes in a way they had never been built before; and the need to hire and train over 40,000 unskilled workers (peak employment was 42,331 in June 1943 with a 15% absenteeism rate), most of whom lived 30 miles away in Detroit and had no expressways to speed them on their way to work; the enormous turnover of people being drafted and others going elsewhere to work (in May 1943, a 56% labor turnover rate was reported for the prior eight months), you begin to comprehend the magnitude of the task.

An examination of Willow Run employment statistics sheds additional light on the enormity of the personnel problems Ford had to overcome (as did all other war manufacturers). When production ended in June 1945, Ford had hired 80,774 people (61% men and 39% women) in the Willow Run plant, of

The B-24 Liberator bomber in unpainted alumiunm. As the war progressed, it was determined that the camouflage paint provided little protection and the added weight of the paint only reduced the speed. (Hudek)

Henry Ford II signing off on the 8,000th B-24 bomber built in March 1945. (HFM 0.16064)

took so long and to appreciate what Ford finally accomplished by the end of the war.

Once production started, Ford made running manufacturing changes to constantly improve the process and save time and money. But, change in the airplane itself proved frustrating in the early days. Ford needed frozen production runs to mass produce planes in the quantities they visualized while the Air Force wanted to make changes every time a report came in from the war zones. Ford finally convinced the Air Force that making batches of planes without significant changes and then, retrofitting them at predetermined times, was the most practical and expeditious method of production. By the end of the war, most plane manufacturers were doing the same.

which only 30,021 stayed over twelve months. 34,533 stayed less than three months with 12,197 quitting in the first ten days. (Only 10,003 men and 317 women left due to being drafted or enlisting in the armed forces.) Employees came from every state and possession of the United States as well as seven foreign countries.

Then add labor troubles, as Ford had just signed their first ever union contract. Stir in nearly daily manufacturing changes to a production process set up to produce the same identical item by the thousands, and you begin to understand why start-up production

Skyways (December 1942) magazine berated Detroit manufacturer's production record while complimenting the old-line aviation industry's record in a major article entitled: *"All-out Ballyhoo versus All-out Production."* Taking particular aim at Ford it stated: *"it was supposed to produce bombers at the unbelievable rate of one an hour - - - where mass production in world record quantities is an every day affair, we find they have failed miserably."* And, by January 1943, with only

56 planes built in all of 1942, the press was calling it: *"Will It Run?"*

But, Ford had not been idle. They had been building components and sending them as knock-down kits, which were more than 80 percent complete, to Consolidated Aircraft in Ft. Worth, Texas, making it possible for them to build 1,142 planes instead of the 350 they had forecasted earlier.

The story of the transportation of these early knock-down kits is worthy of mention, for it illustrates the problems that were solved and economies generated by Ford in satisfying the country's military needs. It was originally planned that these knock-down kits would be shipped by rail. However, rail shipments were much costlier and rail cars were des-

perately needed for other war-related materials. Not only would it require four rail cars per bomber kit, but it would take more time and the sudden impacts and shocks common to rail operations posed the problem of causing hidden damage to fragile airplane assemblies that could later cause structural failure in flight. Special automobile haul-a-way vehicles offered the answer. Two 63 foot trailers, said to be the largest in the world, were designed to haul each complete kit. Each bomber kit was divided into three sections; the aft fuselage section, the nose and the center wing. One trailer carried the fuselage and rudders, while the other carried the wing assembly and other parts. They were pulled by specially designed Toreco tractors powered by two separate 8 cylinder, Mercury 100 hp engines. With an overall length of more than

B-24 knock-down kit. The kits, 90% complete, were shipped to Consolidated Aircraft in Texas and Douglas Aircraft in Oklahoma for final assembly. Ford shipped 1,839 kits by war's end. (Hudek 833.79119.9)

70 feet and loaded weight of about 50,000 pounds spread over eighteen tires, they were designed to negotiate all streets, curbs and underpasses between Michigan and Texas and meet all state axle-loading laws. Operated by two-man crews who alternated driving, each round trip took four days rolling 24 hours a day at an average speed of 40 mph. The result was an 83% savings in time (4 days versus 12) and 67% reduction in cost, while freeing the rail cars to transport other critical war material. Ford continued to send knock-down kits to Consolidated Aircraft in Ft. Worth, Texas and Douglas Aircraft in Tulsa, Oklahoma until July 1944.

Two of these 63 foot trailers were required to transport the sub-assemblies for each plane. This one carried the wing and smaller parts while the other carried the fuselage and rudder. (HFM 833.77899)

By the end of 1942, most problems had been or were in the process of being solved. January 1943 production was 31 planes, February 75, and March reached 104. Although improving, it still took until November 3, 1943 for Ford to build its 1,000th plane. Substantial progress had been made though. Ford Times (November 26, 1943) reported that bomber parts production had been farmed out to virtually every one of Ford's plants and village industries and the War Production Board had announced the Willow Run plant was far above average for efficient utilization of man power, producing 80 pounds gross weight per man, per month, vs. the industry average of 60 pounds per month.

With the arrival of the new year, Ford began producing production miracles. In March 1944, Willow Run, working six days a week on two nine hour shifts, produced 453 planes in 468 hours, one plane every 63 minutes. Nearly 6,000 planes were built in 1944 alone. In late 1944, when Ford was gearing up to build 650 planes a month, or a plane every 45 minutes, priorities changed. With Allied airpower dominating the sky over Europe, bomber fatalities fell, the end of the war in Europe was in view and orders for the B-24 bomber declined. The United States now needed the new long range giant B-29 Superfortress to strike at Japan.

Ford quality was such that the average flight time for complete acceptance of a Ford built

Last B-24 bomber, number 8,685, on June 28, 1945. Henry Ford had his name removed from this plane and let the employees sign their names before shipment. (Hudek)

bomber by the Army was 2 hours and 43 minutes with 39% of the ships accepted on the initial flight. A report made by a Curtiss Wright representative in June 1944 is enlightening: *"Their record delivery day was a ship taking off every three minutes for a period of four hours and for a full day, they delivered 139 planes. The greatest single contributing factor is, all Ford pilots are authorized by Army to accept ships for the Army. Ford is presenting to the Army good, clean airplanes showing high quality workmanship and performance." "For the entire flight area operations there are only 30 - 40 crabs* (problems) *written on each ship. From our point of view, this was phenomenal."* By April 1945, the average crabs had dropped to less than 10 per plane.

The principles with which Ford production people had been indoctrinated proved to be one of the most important of Ford's war time contributions. Ford production attitudes held that any project could be analyzed and improvements made, and accepted ways were always to be challenged. With Ford's manufacturing experience, they felt they could do any job better, faster and cheaper and in fact did improve production methods and save the government money on nearly every defense project they undertook. On the B-24s alone, they had dropped the price from $238,000 in 1942 to $137,000 in 1944. One example suffices to demonstrate the effect of Ford's automated system. Standard assembly methods, as developed by Consolidated, required 250 man hours to dismantle and set up a center wing vertical fixture. The Ford method, using an enormous purpose-built jig, required 2 minutes. With their highly automated machines and assembly line approach, Ford produced nearly fifty percent of all B-24s built.

Willow Run was awarded the coveted Army-Navy E for excellence in May 1945 and the final plane rolled off the line June 28, 1945. The final total showed Ford built 6,792 fly-a-ways and 1,893 knock-down kits, a total of 8,685 planes. The critics had finally been silenced. Today, there are few of these Ford built bombers known to exist.

"War-weary" ladies at Willow Run. Returned from Europe, these bombers would soon be sent to the used plane lot in Arizona. (Hudek 833.81832.2)

In 1945, with the war in Europe over, Ford was called on to handle the war-weary ladies coming back from Europe. The initial contract called for the war-weary B-24s to be flown to Willow Run, stripped of all valuable government equipment such as bombsights, machine guns, photographic equipment, parachutes, life rafts, bombs, ammunition, etc. and then to pickle the planes for storage for future use. Oil was run through the engines and gas lines to prevent rusting. Hydraulic and brake systems, as well as all other moving parts were checked, repaired and coated with suitable preservatives. After half of the 477 ships had been processed, it became obvious these planes would never be needed and the storage arrangements were canceled. Instead, all planes were put in flying condition and flown to a storage facility in Albuquerque, New Mexico. As is now known, virtually all of these planes ended up being sold for insignificant amounts or were destroyed as obsolete.

With the end of hostilities in Europe in May 1945, production of the shorter-range Liberator was canceled in favor of the long-range B-29 Superfortress for missions over Japan. Ford made baffle plates for the B-29's self sealing fuel cells and solved a serious problem for the Hudson Motor Car Company, a

This "weary lady", THAT'S ALL BROTHER completed 83 missions. (Hudek)

prime B-29 contractor. So large were the skin surfaces of the B-29 that the only equipment in Detroit able to roll them were at Ford's Willow Run plant. Ford, naturally, loaned the Willow Run equipment to Hudson to get production underway.

In October, 1941, The Dearborn Press had quoted Henry Ford as saying: *"When the war is over we are going to retain the building we are erecting and construct airplanes on a mass production scale."* He went on to describe his vision of the near future when there would be great fleets of airplanes capable of backyard landings. (He still clung to his dream of an aerial Flivver for the average man.) In November 1943, Ford Times quoted Ford: *"We have been planning for a long time to build a cargo plane at Willow Run after the war."* However, in 1945, his

grandson Henry Ford II, now President of Ford Motor Company which was in dire financial straits, declined to exercise the option to purchase the Willow Run plant.[4] Ford told the employees: *"The company regarded it as designed to meet a temporary need and just as expendable as a battleship."* To the obvious relief of their potential aviation competitors, Ford, being absorbed with saving the Ford Motor Company from financial ruin, never entered the postwar aviation industry.

In 1999, the Ford Motor Company donated $500,000 to the Imperial War Museum, located at Duxford, England to assist in acquiring and restoring a B-24 Liberator bomber. When restoration is completed, it will join a number of other American combat aircraft honoring the United States airmen who served from British bases in World War II.

Aircraft Engines (United States)

Edsel Ford accepted a contract from the Government in June 1940 to produce, under license, 9,000 Rolls-Royce aircraft engines but was overruled by Henry Ford. It was widely reported that Ford, a pacifist, canceled the contract when he discovered that 6,000 of the engines would go to Great Britain. It wasn't until March 8, 1941 that Ford officials explained in a <u>Detroit Free Press</u> article, that Henry Ford didn't answer the pacifist charge at the time because he didn't want to appear to discredit the English engine, which a Ford plant in Great Britain was then producing. They stated the reason for not accepting the Rolls-Royce order was because they felt the engine was obsolete and that Ford never meant he would not produce war material for England. His decision was based on the fact that he believed a new airplane engine of his own design was a superior type that should be used in both British and U.S. military planes. Initial tests showed the Ford engine could develop between 1,500 and 1,700 hp verses the 1,000 hp of the Rolls-Royce.

Many critics have decried this explanation as a cover for Henry Ford's pacifism. Ford, however, had already accepted an aircraft engine contract from the French government. In June 1939, Ford had formed Fordair S.A., a subsidiary of Ford S.A.F. (France), to build 1,200 of the Rolls Royce Merlin X aircraft engines. Most of the production equipment had to be acquired in the United States and efforts were well underway when France fell to the Germans in June 1940. Having had the chance to see the details of the Merlin engine, Ford apparently felt he could do better and it was at this time that he started work on his own airplane engine.

Ford's engine, undertaken without the benefit of a Government contract, was a 12 cylinder, V type, liquid cooled aircraft engine. $2,000,000 later they had developed a 1,650 cubic inch engine developing up to 2,100 hp. However, by the time the engine was developed, a new tank engine was needed more than a new airplane engine and at the government's request, Ford re-engineered this 12 cylinder aircraft engine into an 8 cylinder tank engine. The first production engine built was installed in the first production medium tank off Ford's tank line in May 1942. Over 25,000 of these engines were built and most importantly they raised the average life of a tank engine from 100 hours to 400 hours. Ironically, by September 1943, with heavier tanks needed, Ford was commissioned to develop a 12 cylinder engine patterned on his 8 cylinder tank engine which had been developed from his 12 cylinder airplane engine.

Ford did accept a contract to produce 4,000 Pratt & Whitney aircraft engines and on September 14, 1940, ground was broken in the Rouge complex for a 1,286,344 square foot production facility to build the P & W R-

2800, an 18 cylinder 2000 hp radial engine. Six months later, the building was ready for operation and the first Ford built Pratt & Whitney engine came off the line August 23, 1941. Never the one to waste anything, Ford ran generators off of the engines being tested, generating enough power to meet over 95% of the electrical energy required for the entire building.

Due to the complexity of the engine, which was built from 220 assemblies comprising 11,723 parts, it was necessary to set up an Aircraft Service Department to insure important changes were made after the engines left

One of the first Pratt & Whitney engines built by Ford being packaged for shipment. (Hudek 833.76186)

Ford. Consequently, a Ford field force of 50 men was trained to insure changes were incorporated without delay at ten airplane manufacturers and many Air Force operational bases throughout the United States and overseas. At the same time, an Aircraft Engine Apprentice School was established to train employees and Army Air Corp and Navy personnel.

As in other defense jobs, innovative methods were devised and they cut the time required to build each engine from 2,331 man

hours in November 1942 to 905 by June 1945. The aircraft engine plant employed 23,384 people, built 57,851 engines and earned the Army Navy E for excellence. Also awarded the coveted "E" for exceptional production of aircraft engine parts was the Ford plant in Minneapolis, Minnesota.

In an arrangement that seemed to defy logic, rather than have Ford build an engine that fit the B-24 bomber in their airplane engine plant, in the Rouge, 25 miles east of Willow Run, Ford's contract was for engines which were shipped all over the United States. Conversely, the engines used in the Ford built bomber were Pratt & Whitney 14 cylinder, 1,250 hp engines built hundreds of miles away by Buick (Melrose Park, Illinois), Chevrolet (Buffalo, New York), and Pratt & Whitney (East Hartford, Connecticutt). The Ford engines produced at the Rouge were used in the Curtiss C-46, Douglas A-26, Martin B-26, Northrop P-61, Republic P-47 and Vega B-34 airplanes.

Aircraft Engines (England)

In March 1940, Ford started construction in Manchester, England of a factory to produce Rolls Royce Merlin V-12 airplane engines. As in the United States, Ford was starting from scratch in finding employees and obtaining the necessary but scarce machinery, however in war time England, the task was greatly magnified. They could not take qualified people from other plants and in the end, women accounted for 43% of the employees. Ford engineers found the design tolerances for the Merlin engines to be much greater than Ford allowed for their automobile engines. Ford reworked the drawings to much finer tolerances and in June 1941, the first Ford built Merlin came off the line. Production targets called for 400 engines a month costing £5,640 each. By September 1942, the target was exceeded and, again due to Ford production methods, the cost dropped to £1,875. By mid 1944, monthly production was over 900 units a month at a cost of just

£1,200. Ford turned in a magnificent performance building over 30,000 engines and not one failed the stringent acceptance tests of the Royal Air Force. Most of the engines were MkXX models used primarily in the Lancaster bombers and the Beaufighter, Defiant, Halifax and Hurricane fighters.

In addition, by the end of the war, 56 airfields in Great Britain had been constructed of a product called Tarmacadam, manufactured from the slag produced by Ford's blast furnaces.

High Altitude Test Flying

A number of lesser contracts were let for various types of testing and problem solving. One of the more important of these contracts approved in February 1943, authorized Ford to conduct high altitude flights to test the General Electric ignition system designed for the Pratt & Whitney R-2800 engines. The tests called for a minimum of 55 hours at an altitude of not less than 35,000 feet.

Using a Republic P-47D Thunderbolt, powered by the R-2800 engine, tests were conducted by Charles Lindbergh, then a Ford Motor Company technical advisor, and other Ford pilots. These tests contributed invaluable data on the operation of ignition systems and engine performance at extreme altitudes.

The initial test flight, run October 19, 1942

First CG-4A glider finishing flight test at Ford Airport. Test pilot commented that it was the best glider he had flown. (Hudek 822.77508)

by Lindbergh, reached a maximum height of 36,000 feet. The highest altitude of all these tests was 43,020 feet, reached on December 29, 1943, in the Thunderbolt. Again, it was Lindbergh at the controls, who by this time had flown more than 20 hours over 36,000 feet.

In addition, considerable other technical data on high altitude engine performance was obtained and it was some of these experiences that Lindbergh was later able to share with our fighter pilots in the Pacific Theater of Operation.

Ford also developed the most advanced altitude chamber in the world for simultaneously simulating temperatures to 100° below zero and altitudes to 60,000 feet. The chamber was used for testing equipment and training up to 14 men at a time to meet the emergencies that could arise at high altitudes.

Gliders

Prior to 1940, all automobiles required a great deal of wood in the manufacturing process, and this demand for wood and Ford's desire for control over his raw materials led him to Michigan's Upper Peninsula. In 1919, Ford purchased over 700,000 acres of land and in 1921 established a sawmill at Iron Mountain, Michigan.[5] Over the years, Ford employed a large number of woodworking craftsmen in his operations, and by 1940, most of the work was centered on the wooden bodies for Ford's *Woody* stationwagon. With the attack on Pearl Harbor in December 1941, most of the plant was closed and unemployment in the area soared, forcing these trained craftsmen to leave for jobs in the cities booming with war work. The only remaining work at the Ford plant, which required few employees, was making the large wooden shipping containers for the Pratt & Whitney engines being built at Ford's Rouge plant in Dearborn, Michigan. The glider contracts to be awarded Ford would bring many of the craftsmen back home again.

While Germany had been prohibited from creating an Air Force by the terms of the Armistice ending World War I, they found that interest in aviation could be encouraged by creating gliding clubs. These clubs were subsidized by the German government and the they started training schools for glider pilots, they contracted with the Waco Aircraft Co. to design and produce the mostly wooden CG-4A glider capable of carrying 15 men, or a Jeep or a howitzer. But additional production capacity was needed and a number of manufacturers were awarded glider contracts. In March 1942, Ford was approached by the Army to build the Waco glider and realized it would be a perfect use for their nearly idle plant at Iron Mountain and a lifesaver for the local community. Six months later in September 1942, the first Ford glider, a prototype built at Ford Airport in Dearborn, was towed into the air to be test flown by an Army glider pilot. For 15 minutes, the glider

First of the larger CG-13A gliders following test flight at Ford Airport, Dearborn, Michigan. (Hudek 833.79186.16)

glider pilots later formed the basis of the German Luftwaffe in the mid 1930s. The Germans made use of their glider expertise in the 1940 invasion of Holland and Belgium, utilizing ten-man gliders to land troops 20 miles behind the lines. In May 1941, they again used gliders in their successful conquest of the Island of Crete.

The American military was well aware of these successful German operations and, as was put through a grueling series of maneuvers. When the ship landed, the pilot reported it to be the best they had flown. The highest tribute possible.

In that six months between March and September, Ford negotiated a contract for the first one thousand CG-4A gliders with the Army, and obtained a set of Waco's blueprints that had to be enlarged to accommodate Ford's mass production methods. In addition, they had to design, purchase and/or produce non-existing tooling and rework the Iron Mountain facility for the new glider program.

In lofting or enlarging the Waco drawings to full scale, Ford found that Waco engineers had been overwhelmed with the rush of government business and hadn't been able to record many of the changes made on the shop floor resulting in about 1,200 of Ford's 2,000 full scale drawings being scrapped. Ford also re-designed the structure of many parts of the glider in order to simplify, improve and strengthen the ship. As a result, of the 12,000 engineering changes later issued by the government, only 1,000 applied to Ford. Due to the lack of special steel making facilities at Ford's Iron Mountain plant, the steel fuselage frame was sub-contracted to the Lloyd Manufacturing Co. in nearby Menominee, Michigan. Because of the consistent high quality of these gliders, Ford was granted a Quality A Control Rating, which meant that Ford inspected its own work with only spot checks by government inspectors. In addition, Ford was appointed the prime engineering contractor, vested with the responsibility for making all revisions and improvements for all contractors.

From the beginning of production, Ford insisted on assembling all gliders as though for test-flight, and then dismantled them for crating. As a result, Army personnel at glider bases reported that Ford gliders were the only ones which could be readily reassembled. All contractors were subsequently required to do the same pre-assembly. In addition, Ford construction methods were so accurate that a Ford glider was sent to each of the other contractors to be used as a standard for interchangeability of parts.

While the first 110 CG-4A gliders were to be flight delivered from Ford Airport in nearby Kingsford, Michigan for delivery in the United States for training purposes, the short runway and winter weather required them to be broken down and trucked to Dearborn for re-assembly. They were then towed to their destinations to be used as training ships for a newly formed Army unit called Winged Commandos. Later, the Army developed a system for towing the gliders from the short runway at Ford Airport. Army C-47s (military versions of the Douglas DC-3) snatched up two gliders at a time from the ground and delivered them to various glider training schools. The balance of the glider production was crated and shipped by rail.

Although the Army's contract called for test flights of one unit in 20, all of the first 110 Ford gliders were flight tested before being delivered to the Army. As this represented more than 10% of the original contract, Ford was not required to test-flight additional units. The quality of Ford gliders was such that Army Air Force personnel stated the Ford units had been found to stand up well under the minimum requirement of 500 hours of training flight operations without repairs and in most instances they lasted 2,000 hours.

Material shortages delayed the delivery of the first Iron Mountain gliders until December 1942 when four units were built. January saw 17 completed, 44 in February, 78 in March and then an average of 127 a month until the peak of 216 was reached in March 1945. Production ceased in August 1945.

The CG-4A could be towed at 150 mph and had a gliding speed of 65 mph. It was 48 feet 4 inches long with a wingspan of 83 feet, 8 inches and weighed up to 9,000 pounds loaded.

After the Allied Invasion of Sicily, in which the CG-4A was used, the Army saw the need for a larger ship and in June 1943, Ford received a contract for 50 semi-experimental larger CG-13A gliders, capable of carrying 30 fully equipped men (later increased to 42) or two Jeeps or a howitzer and one Jeep with crew and ammunition. The first unit was built in the Airframe Building in the Rouge plant in Dearborn and test flown in December 1943. The remaining units were built in the Iron Mountain plant.

The CG-13A could be towed at 200 mph. Only slightly larger than the CG-4A, with a length of 54 feet 4 inches and a wingspan of 85 feet 7 inches, the loaded weight jumped to 15,000 pounds.

Again, as with other war production con-tracts, costs were substantially reduced as Ford engineers found better and faster ways of production. One major innovation that illustrates this point was the use of a gluing fixture that reduced drying time from eight hours to ten minutes. (This process, considered a secret, was furnished to the British for use in their Mosquito bombers that had a plywood stressed fuselage.) As a result of production and design improvements, the cost of building the small CG-4A glider dropped from $21,391 to $12,159 and the cost of the large CG-13A glider dropped from $62,202 to $30,276.[6] Ford had become the largest producer of gliders, building 4,202 CG-4A models and 87 of the CG-13A models.

In addition to the gliders and shipping crates for the gliders and aircraft engines, the Iron Mountain plant made oak flooring and tables for the Willow Run bomber plant as well as miscellaneous wood products for other defense needs.

On June 21, 1944, the Iron Mountain plant and its workers received the coveted "Army Navy E" award for excellence in production.

Jet Bomb Engine

In mid 1944, Ford was asked to build a jet engine based on specifications contained in a sketchy five page Allied Command report. The report vaguely described the construction details of the German V-1 robot engines used to power the terror bomb over England.

Jet engine for Army and Navy missiles was a copy of the German V-1. Plans were being made to produce 1,000 engines a day for use against Japan when World War II ended. (Hudek 833.80765.3)

A short time later, Ford engineers were able to examine the badly mutilated engine parts of a dud bomb that had impacted the earth at 400 mph and had been rushed from England to Wright Field, Dayton, Ohio. Ford had been offered this contract based on their World War I experiments with the Buzz Bomb and the recognized success of their engineering and mass production of aircraft engines and other precision equipment. In July 1944, Ford was awarded a contract for 25 prototype jet engines to be used with a robot aerial bomb: code named MX-544. These engines were designed to fly for two hours with enough power to drive the engine and plane with a bomb load at 400 mph.

In three weeks, the first Ford jet engine was successfully operated at the Rouge plant and by October 1944, the first three engines built. Designated PJ-31-1, they were tested and accepted by the Air Force, eliminating the necessity of building the other 22 units. These three units, produced at the Rouge complex, led to an initial production order for 3,000 engines. The importance to the Air Force of this secret weapon is attested to by the fact that, subject to testing the tactical use of the bomb against Japan, Ford was asked to submit facilities requirement data for building 100 units a day; then 500 units a day; then 1,000 units a day. However, only 2,400 engines were actually produced by the time the contract was canceled on VJ day (August 14, 1945). These engines were designed to be used to power three types of missiles: the Air Force JB-2 and JB-10 and the Navy's Loon, with the JB-2 and Loon being substantially improved versions of the German V-1 buzz bomb. None were ever used in combat.

Other Production

Ford designed and developed a Quick Change Power Plant for the Republic P-47D airplane which allowed for the complete removal of the power plant and installation of an identical power plant ready for operation in 24 minutes compared to the 40 hours normally required to change power plants in planes of this type. In addition, Ford trained 50,000 Army and Navy personnel in various aviation courses, as well as other needed mechanical specialties at schools at Willow Run and the Rouge plants. They also produced 7,053 bomb trucks, 17,008 jettisonable gas tanks, 87,390 aircraft generators and 5,360 rate-of-climb indicators.

Chapter 14 - Notes

(1) The Ford Archives contains a number of telegrams covering Ford's attempt to get a German plane with a Mercedes engine. In addition, he talks about his intention to build 150,000 airplanes for use in France by the U.S. Government. (Ford Archives, Accession 1, Box 12). *(page 163)*

(2) Bill Stout designed a small single seat *Cootie* airplane in 1919 to use the 2 cylinder *Buzz Bomb* engine. It never developed more than half of its rated horsepower and as a result, Stout's *Cootie* never flew. *(page 164)*

(3) Ford had owned much of the property since 1931 and had established Camp Willow Run there to help sons of dead and disabled World War I veterans to get a start in life. *(page 169)*

(4) Following the end of World War II, airport operations at Willow Run continued in use serving as the main airport terminal for metropolitan Detroit. In late 1958, all remaining passenger service was transferred to Wayne County Airport (now Detroit Metro). Airport production facilities that had cost the government $100,000,000 were sold to the new Kaiser-Frazer Motor Car Company for $15,000,000. *(page 176)*

(5) The sawmill operation at Iron Mountain generated an enormous amount of waste, something Henry Ford could not abide. As a result, a chemical plant was erected in 1924 to produce wood distillation products from waste wood. One of the most well known of these products was the charcoal briquettes developed and sold by Ford for commercial and home use for years. By 1944, Ford produced 75% of the nation's charcoal which was a regulated product required for essential wartime uses. In 1951, the charcoal operation along with the rest of the plant, was sold to the Kingsford Chemical Company. The Kingsford Briquette, with the Ford story printed on the back of the bag, is one of the most popular brands on the market today. *(page 180)*

(6)   The cost figures given are from Ford Motor Company records immediately following the war. Army Air Force Glider Program Study #217 in 1947, reported that Ford gliders cost $14,956 per unit versus $18,659 for Waco, the next lowest and $21,800 for General, the highest. *(page 183)*

15

THE LEGACY

As the 20th century ended, a search was on for the various individuals and events that most influenced and defined the years since 1900. Henry Ford was selected by <u>Forbes</u> magazine and numerous other organizations as the businessman of the century and his Model T automobile was selected as the car of the century. All Ford's nominations and acclamations were based on a combination of events surrounding the Model T that had happened during the first quarter of the century; Henry Ford's fixation with low-cost transportation for the public, his application of the moving assembly line to automobile production, the $5.00 day for employees so that they could buy what they produced and so on. No one, however, has even mentioned his contribution to civil aviation.

Just as Ford recognized the potential influence of motorized ground transportation on the life of the average individual, and designed and priced his product for them, especially the farmer, so too did he foresee the impact of aviation. He was so fascinated by the German *Zeppelin's* endurance and load-carrying capacity demonstrated during World War I, that he sent Bill Mayo to Europe to investigate the potential for production in the United States. He offered to build a similar airship for the United States Navy and, although failing to interest the Navy, he was so convinced of the future of the airship that he built the first privately owned dirigible mooring mast in the world when there were only three airships, all military, in the United States to utilize it.

He and his son Edsel continued to follow the development of aviation through the early 1920s watching the barnstormers excite the public while, at the same time, convincing them that flying was for reckless daredevils. Ford, along with others, knew that in order for aviation to come of age, the public had to be convinced of its safety and reliability. He watched with interest, Bill Stout's experiments with his all-metal Air Sedan and Air Pullman aircraft. Finally, he felt the time was ripe for taming aviation in the minds of the public and that Bill Stout's all-metal airplane provided the best opportunity.

Without diminishing the importance of his early interest in airships and airplanes and the influence it had on him in the succeeding years, 1925 stands out as the beginning of Henry and Edsel Ford's aviation legacy. In

January, Ford Airport was dedicated. In April, he started the Ford Air Transportation Service as an experimental and demonstration airline. In August, he purchased the Stout Metal Airplane Company to manufacture airplanes and in October, he was the main sponsor of the first National Air Tour to demonstrate to the public the safety and reliability of commercial aviation. Also in October, he sold his first airplane and in November, his first three-engine airship was flown.

Henry Ford was in a unique position. He not only had an enormous fortune and absolute ownership of the Ford Motor Company, which allowed him to follow his instincts but he also had an extraordinarily positive public image. With the introduction of the Model T in 1908, he had freed the farmer and the average man from the restrictions of the horse and buggy and as methods of production improved and volume increased, he drove the price of his car down: from $850 in 1908 to $290 in 1925 so the average man could afford a car. As a result, he could do no wrong as far as the majority of the public was concerned. In 1924, Henry Ford and his son Edsel committed themselves to aviation by building a brand new factory designed for manufacturing airplanes, something unheard of in those days, and constructed what was at the time considered the finest airport in the United States. In order to convince a skeptical public, Henry Ford, utilizing Stout's single engine all-metal plane, formed the Ford Air Transportation Service in 1925 as a

demonstration air service. His air service was the first to fly on a predictable daily schedule, subject only to weather and mechanical delays. He was the first private operator to fly the U.S. Air Mail, furthering his efforts to prove that scheduled air service could be provided in a safe and reliable manner. Once in operation, all information derived from his experience was made available and his first catalog featured chapters on How to Organize an Air Line and General Information About The Landing Field.

Henry Ford's activities were not happening in a vacuum. He was operating against a background of government activities that had been simmering for years. Legislation to control and license commercial aviation had been recommended as early as 1918, and bills were introduced in Congress every following year until the Air Commerce Act was passed in 1926. A companion to these efforts, again started in 1918, had been the effort to expand the Air Mail service which culminated with the passage of the Air Mail Act of 1925, directing the Post Office to contract for the carriage of domestic mail with commercial contractors. The impact of these laws was not readily perceived by the public but those interested in aviation were aware of these efforts and that certainly included Henry Ford who had anticipated them when he staked Bill Stout to his factory and an airport.

The mere fact that Henry Ford took aviation seriously convinced many businessmen that this air game must be a serious business. But most of the public still had to be convinced that flying was anything but a fool's game. Between 1927 and 1932, Ford spent $558,697[1] advertising in all major aviation magazines as well as other general publications, such as National Geographic, Literary Digest, Time and Saturday Evening Post. The combined circulation of the magazines was over six million, reaching an estimated fifteen to twenty million people in the United States. He also advertised in most of the major daily newspapers, reaching untold additional millions. These ads, while extolling the virtues of the all-metal Ford plane, were also aimed at publicizing the safety and reliability of aviation with such headlines as: *"Safety Wins the Traffic"*, *"Lift Up Your Eyes"*, *"Nothing Can Take the Place of Safety"*, *"Tireless Wings"*, *"When Women Fly"*, *"Ford Trained Pilots for Ford Planes"* and *"The Highways of the Sky."*

Ironically, in the late 1920s and 1930s, his own all-metal Tri-Motor would be used by a number of barnstormers but with a difference. The Ford name and the all-metal, three-engine plane now represented safety in flight instead of the daredevil antics of pilots in wood and fabric planes just a few years before. Many thousands of Americans took their first flight in a Ford Tri-Motor and even the most reluctant spectator allowed as how the Ford plane looked safe.

Once Henry Ford was convinced of the worth of an idea, he spared no expense in developing it. As fine as his airport was, Ford planes could not take off with full loads on muddy and rutted runways and they suffered flight restrictions imposed by inclement weather. To overcome these problems, and no doubt the jibes of the local press in referring to his airport as *Lake Ford*, he had the first concrete runways in the world installed. So revolutionary was this that the Smithsonian referred to it as Ford's greatest contribution to aviation. Equally important was Ford engineers' development of a radio system that allowed accurate flying in stormy weather, increasing the dependability and safety of scheduled air operations and is the bedrock of commercial aviation today. Compounding the importance of these developments, was the fact that Henry Ford never claimed a royalty on any of his aviation patents and freely shared his aviation production and air service operational experiences with interested parties.

Henry Ford, realizing the need for transient quarters for the airborne traveler, built the Dearborn Inn, the finest and one of the first hotels in the nation dedicated to the airline passenger.

Also during this period, Edsel Ford was promoting aerial exploration of the polar regions. He was an early backer of the Wilkins' expedition and the most influential backer of the Byrd expeditions. He not only made substantial cash and material contributions, but also solicited funds from other industrialists. Byrd wrote Edsel ford: *"The whole thing would have been impossible without you."*

Henry Ford anticipated the Post Office Department's drive to make the airmail pay for itself by making passenger service carry the majority of overhead expenses. Even while starting his airline with Stout's small plane in early 1925, Ford knew that commercial aviation would need bigger planes carrying bigger payloads if profitable operations were to be achieved. Early on, he envisioned 100 passenger aircraft and shortly after buying the Stout Metal Airplane Company, he directed efforts towards a three-engine airplane — greater size for greater capacity and more engines for greater safety and reliability. Following Charles Lindbergh's dramatic New York to Paris flight, Henry Ford commented: *"I am interested in large planes — real planes, planes that will carry 100 to 200 passengers, planes that will fly in any kind of weather, in any season of the year. Planes that will go anywhere anytime. If one man can fly across the ocean, 100 men can be carried across the ocean with passenger planes."* (Cleveland Plain Dealer, May 28, 1927).

In 1926, Ford declared that he would build nothing but all-metal three-engine planes at a time when there were no other all-metal planes in the United States and only the Fokker, a wooden-winged, fabric covered plane, offered a three-engine aircraft with

similar passenger capacity, but Fokker also continued building his single engine planes. To this end, Ford established the assembly line method of producing airplanes when every other manufacturer was building them by hand, one at a time.

The all-metal, three-engine Ford airplane, backed by the Ford name and advertising, revolutionized the public's conception of safety in air travel. Ford airplanes dominated the airline industry until Ford relinquished the business to the Boeing 247s and Douglas DC-2s and 3s in the mid 1930s.

The Smithsonian Institute, in its catalog of aircraft in the museum, summed up the impact of Henry Ford and the Ford Tri-Motor on commercial aviation quite simply: *"One of the most important events in the selling of aviation to the general public was the entry of Henry Ford into aircraft manufacturing. The Ford automobile was at the time the symbol of reliability and it followed in the minds of a good many people that a Ford airplane would be safe to fly. And it was. The Ford Tri-Motor was a rugged, dependable transport airplane, which won a permanent place in aviation history."*[2]

A confirmed pacifist who thought war was for politicians and greedy industrialists, he was attacked, belittled and ridiculed by the press. Once the United States declared itself as a participant, he quickly directed the enormous productive facilities of his company towards the war effort, unleashing the tremendous pool of talent that had created his automotive empire. In virtually every war contract undertaken, Ford managers, designers and workers devised ways to improve quality and increase production, while at the same time driving down contracted costs. Nowhere was this more evident than in the introduction of the assembly line approach towards building Liberator bombers and the troop carrying gliders. Having originally introduced the assembly line method to build his Tri-Motor airplane in the 1920s, he found airplane manufacturers in the 1940s still hand building airplanes one at a time. He would once again revolutionize airplane production by precision construction of the Liberator bomber on the assembly line. By continuously improving construction methods, Ford achieved his often ridiculed goal of building one of these massive airplanes every hour.

Henry Ford's influence is felt today through his pioneering promotional efforts and his innovative ideas about aviation, such as the assembly line production of aircraft, the radio beacon, concrete runways, airplane brakes and tailwheels to name a few. Henry Ford had developed an organization that created the first air service in the United States that actually ran on schedule. They built 212 aircraft of different types and sizes, developing many innovative techniques for manufacturing planes in a manner that had never been made before. Virtually every major American airline, or their predecessor, started with Ford Tri-Motor airplanes in their inventory.

His aviation venture has been criticized by some as a whim that cost in excess of $11,000,000. That figure shrinks considerably when the value of the land and buildings still in use is subtracted, and no one has bothered to calculate the value of the nearly 13,000,000 pounds of freight carried to his various plants by his Air Transportation Service, nor what effect emergency air shipments had on keeping those assembly lines running.

Yet aviation books and magazine articles continue to appear where the authors are unaware of, or make little mention of, the avaition achievements of Henry and Edsel Ford.

In April 1984, Henry Ford was enshrined in the National Aviation Hall of Fame in Dayton, Ohio, a fitting tribute to one of the great pioneers of commercial aviation in the United States.

Notes - Chapter 15

(1) Ford spent an additional $3,242,000 in promotion. It is not possible to determine how much was truly promotion and how much was developmental, as 1931 is the only year for which there is some detail. For instance, included in the $1,200,000 for promotion in 1931 was $110,439 for loss of the XB906 bomber and $500,000 for developmental work on the 14AT. *(page 189)*

(2) *Aircraft of the National Air and Space Museum,* 1985, Smithsonian Institution Press. *(page 190)*

APPENDIX

FORD AIR TRANSPORTATION SERVICE STATISTICS

Schedule	Inaugurated	Terminated
Dearborn - Chicago	Apr 13, 1925	Aug 6, 1932
Dearborn - Cleveland	Jul 1, 1925	Jul 19, 1928
Dearborn - Cleveland	Mar 10, 1930	Apr 9, 1932
Dearborn - Buffalo	Mar 26, 1927	Mar 10, 1930
Cleveland - Buffalo	Mar 10, 1930	Jan 12, 1931

	Dearborn Chicago	Dearborn Cleveland	Cleveland Buffalo	Dearborn Buffalo	Total
Trips Scheduled	4,395	3,586	460	1,708	10,149
Trips Completed	4,115	3,435	420	1,473	9,443
% COMPLETED	94	96	91	86	93
Trips canceled (mainly weather)	134	109	35	208	486
Forced landings:					
Weather	107	29	5	21	162
Mechanical	39	13	0	6	58

(30 of the 58 mechanical failures were with 2ATs in first two years of Air Transport operations.)

	Dearborn Chicago	Dearborn Cleveland	Cleveland Buffalo	Dearborn Buffalo	Total
Flying hours	10,644	4,799	805	4,055	20,265
Miles flown	993,108	44,222	84,711	356,344	1,878,385
Freight (000 #)	5,655	4,459	731	1,965	12,810

FORD AIRPLANE STATISTICS

Ford Airplane Designations

2AT	Eight person aircraft, powered by single Liberty engine.
3AT	Modified version of 2AT powered by three Wright J-4 engines.
4AT-A	Twelve passenger aircraft powered by three Wright J-4 engines. Six other 4AT models used different engine combinations.
5AT-A	Fourteen passenger aircraft powered by Pratt & Whitney Wasp engines. Four other 5AT models used different engine combinations.
6AT	5AT airframe powered by Wright J-6 engines.
7AT	Modified 6AT powered by Pratt & Whitney engines.
8AT	5AT airframe powered by single engine.
9AT	4AT airframe powered by three Pratt & Whitney Wasp Jr. engines.
10AT	Model of 32 passenger airplane powered by four Pratt & Whitney engines.
11AT	4AT airframe powered by three Packard diesel engines.
12AT	Model of 32 passenger airplane powered by Hispano-Suiza engine on center mounted pedestal with two Pratt & Whitney engines in wings.

13AT 5AT airframe powered by two Wright J-6 and one Wright Cyclone engines.
14AT Thirty two passenger aircraft powered by three Hispano-Suiza engines.
15AT Model of fourteen passenger, twin engine aircraft.
15P Two seat flying wing powered by Ford aluminum V8 engine.

Air Transport 2AT Production

There has been much confusion as to how many 2ATs were built and their serial numbers. A letter dated August 4, 1927, from Stout's office to F. L. Black, Ford Advertising Manager, recapping planes produced to that date, lists planes with serial numbers 2 through 6 as purchased by Ford Motor Company (number 1 had been sold to the Post Office), number 7 as purchased by the Wanamaker Company and numbers 8 through 11 as purchased by Florida Airways. Three 2ATs under construction were destroyed in the January 1926 fire that engulfed Stout's factory. The next eight planes listed are 4AT Tri-Motors, with the ill-fated 3AT being conveniently forgotten. Ford purchase orders to the Stout Metal Airplane Company for the first four planes have been found and state these planes were the 2nd, 3rd, 4th and 5th serial numbered Stout airplanes.

Ford Airplane Production by year and type

Year	2AT	3AT	4AT	5AT	8AT	14AT	X Planes	Total
1925	6	1						7
1926			2				1	3
1927			12				3	15
1928			38	17				55
1929			25	68	1			94
1930				10				10
1931			1	19				20
1932				3		1		4
1933				2				2
1936							1	1
1945							1	1
Total	6	1	78	119	1	1	6	212

Comparison Specifications

	2AT	5AT	DC-3
Wing Span	58'4"	77'10"	95'
Length	45'8"	50'3"	64'5"
Empty Weight (lbs)	3,638	7,600	16,000
Passengers	6	14	21
Cruising Speed (mph)	100	122	191

Ford's Aviation Expenditures

Land & depreciated value of buildings and equipment, May 31, 1932	$ 3,475,568
Inventory, May 31, 1932	1,266,242
Losses, 1925 - 1931	5,627,996
Estimated losses Jan '32 - Aug '33	1,000,000
Total	**$11,369,825**

This total expenditure equates to over $114,000,000 in current dollars.

Memorabilia

AIRPLANE FACTORY BADGE. Worn by management and hourly workers in the Ford Tri-Motor airplace factory.

AIRLINE TIMETABLES - Stout Air Lines timetable, April 1,1928. Stout was the first to use Ford Tri-Motors in passenger service. Stout Air Lines eventually became part of United Air Lines. Maddux Air Lines timetable, late 1927. Maddux Air Lines was the second passenger carrier to use Ford planes and later became part of TWA.

NO FORD PLANE HAS EVER WORN OUT

A VISIT TO THE FORD AIRPORT

NOW THAT MAN HAS WINGS
HE FLIES — NO POWER IN THE
WORLD CAN HOLD HIM BACK

Ford Airport was considered the finest in the United States and the equal of any airport in the world when dedicated in 1925.

One of the Ford brochures and pamphlets proclaiming the durability of the Tri-Motor.

FLY to CLEVELAND

SAVE TIME

An early Stout Air Line timetable featurng a crude drawing of a Ford Tri-Motor.

Maddux Air Line postcard advertising their many routes in late 1928.

Inman Brothers Flying Circus postcard. Reverse side advertises rides for 50¢ in the morning and $1.00 in the afternoon.

Virtually every major airline used Ford Tri-Motor planes. American Airways timetable December 1, 1931; United Air Lines timetable July 15, 1931; and TWA timetable December 1, 1932.

PANAGRA airlines sight seeing pamphlet 1930's.

SOUVENIR TICKET
of Airplane Flight in
Ford Tri-Motored Plane "Miss Albany"
ALL-FORD DAYS at WATERTOWN AIRPORT
AUGUST 23-24-25
GEO. G. "SLIM" EMERSON, Pilot
P. W. DEVENDORF CORP., WATERTOWN

MILUO & WHALING INC.   MURRY MOTOR CAR CO.
CARTHAGE   ADAMS
                              CEO. O. GILLICK
№ 495   CLAYTON

SOUVENIR OF FLIGHT
IN TRI-MOTORED
FORD-STOUT ALL-METAL AIRPLANE
NAME *John D. Kellogg*
Thurs. Aug. 8 1929.
TRI-MOTORED AIR TOURS, INC.

TICKET STUBS such as these were saved as cherished souvenirs of people's first airplane ride.

A rare collection of World War II memorabilia from one Ford employee. Earl Albertson was a senior purchasing manager for Ford. Left to right is Albertson's factory badge for Willow Run; laminated identification card; Willow Run Army Navy E Award program; and Albertson's personal E Award card and pin.

One of many catalogs and training manuals issued by Ford to train the thousands of new employees.

Picture badges were required for all employees in defense plants during World War II. Badge on left was for Mead Bricker, General Manager of the Willow Run plant. Badge on right was for a Government employee assigned to the Aircraft Engine Department at the Rouge. Side cutouts on badges were color keyed to specific departments in a plant.

TEMPORARY AND TRAINING BADGES. Left to right: Navy School badge for aircraft engine training at the Rouge. Army School badge for B-24 training at Willow Run and a Willow Run Trainee badge.

REFERENCES

General

Archives, U.S. Postal Service, Washington, DC

Baron, Robert, papers, Dearborn Historical Museum, Dearborn, MI

Ford Film Collection, National Archives, Washington, DC

Ford Industrial Archives, Dearborn, MI

Knauss, Stanley, papers, Burton Historical Society, Detroit Public Library, Detroit, MI

Research Center, Dearborn Historical Museum, Dearborn, MI

Research Center, Henry Ford Museum & Greenfield Village, Dearborn, MI

Books

Allen, Hugh, *The Story of The Airship,* 1931 (The Goodyear Tire & Rubber Co., Akron, OH)

Carr, Charles, *ALCOA, An American Enterprise*, 1952 (Rinehart & Co, Inc, NY)

Curtis Publishing Co, *The Aviation Industry, A Study of Underlying Trends*, 1930 (The Curtis Publishing Co, Philadelphia, PA)

Davies, R. E. G., *Airlines of the United States Since 1914*, (Smithsonian Institution Press, Washington, DC)

Dickey III, Philip, *The Liberty Engine*, 1968 (Smithsonian Institution Press, Washington, DC)

Dierkx, Marc, *Fokker*, 1997 (Smithsonian Institution Press, Washington, DC)

Duke, Donald, *Airports and Airways*, 1927 (The Ronald Press Company, NY)

Forden, Leslie, *The Ford Air Tours*, 1972 (The Nottingham Press, Alameda, CA)

Hallion, Richard, *Legacy Of Flight*, 1977 (University of Washington Press, Seattle, WA)

Hanks, Stedman, *International Airports*, 1929 (The Ronald Press, NY)

Holmes, Donald, *Air Mail, An Illustrated History 1793-1981*, 1981 (Clarkson N. Potter, NY)

Hotson, Fred, *The Bremen*, 1988 (Canav Books, Toronto, Canada)

Komons, Nick, *Bonfires to Beacons*, 1977 (Smithsonian Institution Press, Washington, DC)

Kuhn, Arthur, *GM Passes Ford 1918-1938*, 1986 (The Pennsylvania State University Press, University Park, MD)

Larkins, William, *The Ford Tri-Motor 1926 - 1992*, 1992, (Schiffer Publishing Ltd, West Chester, PA.)

Lewis, David, *The Public Image of Henry Ford*, 1976, (Wayne State University Press, Detroit, MI)

Lindbergh, Charles, *The Wartime Journals of Charles Lindbergh*, 1970 (Harcourt Brace Jovanovich Inc, NY)

Lipsner, Benjamin, *The Airmail, Jennies to Jets*, 1951 (Wilcox & Follett Co, Chicago, IL)

Meyer, Robert, *Aviation Milestones, Smithsonian Institution*, 1991 (Smithsonian Institution Press, Washington, DC)

Nevins & Hill, *Ford: Expansion & Challenge 1915-1933,* 1957 (Charles Scribner's Sons, NY)

Nevins & Hill, *Ford: Decline and Rebirth 1933-1962*, 1963 (Charles Scribner's Sons, NY)

O'Callaghan, Timothy, *Henry Ford's Airport and Other Aviation Ventures 1909 - 1954*, 1995 (Proctor Publications, Ann Arbor, MI)

Rhode, Bill, *Bailing Wire, Chewing Gum and Guts*, 1970 (Kennikat Press, Port Washington, NY)

Robinson, Douglas, *Giants In The Sky, A History of the Rigid Airship*, 1976 (University of Washington Press, Seattle, WA)

Roseberry, C.R., *The Challenging Skies*, 1966 (Doubleday & Co, Garden City, NY)

Saunders, Hilary St. George, *Ford At War*, 1946 (Private Publication, Great Britain)

Smith, Harry, *Airways*, 1942 (Alfred A. Knopf, NY)

Sorensen, Charles, *My Forty Years With Ford*, 1956 (W. W. Norton & Co, Inc, NY)

Stout, William, *So Away I Went*, 1951 (The Bobs Merrille Co, Inc, NY)

Van Schiever, Thomas, *The History of Ford Air Transportation*, 1980 (VIP Printing, St. Louis, MO)

Significant Magazine Articles

Bombard, Owen, *The Tin Goose*, The Dearborn Historian, 1958

Bryan, Ford, *Dearborn's Buzz Bomb Engine*, The Dearborn Historian, 1991

Hagelthorn, Richard, *Dearborn's "Spruce Goose,"* The Dearborn Historian, 1982

Neville, John, *Ford Aviation* (series of eight articles), Aviation, 1929

Sherman, Don, *Willow Run*, Air & Space, 1992

Thaden, Herbert, *210 Ft. Airship Mooring Tower at Detroit Airport*, Engineering News, 1924

Selected articles from following magazines:

Aero Digest
Automotive Industries
Aviation
Literary Digest
Popular Aviation

Selected articles from following newspapers:

Army & Navy Journal
Dearborn Press, Dearborn, MI
Detroit Free Press, Detroit, MI
Detroit News, Detroit, MI
Detroit Times, Detroit, MI
Ford News (employee newspaper)
Grand Rapids Press, Grand Rapids, MI
Herald American, Syracuse, NY
New York Post, New York, NY
New York Times, New York, NY
New York World, New York, NY
Pontiac News, Pontiac, MI
Pontiac Press, Pontiac, MI

INDEX